On Board for More
World
Adventures

Scott Berlin   Megumi Kobayashi

KINSEIDO

Kinseido Publishing Co., Ltd.

3-21 Kanda Jimbo-cho, Chiyoda-ku,
Tokyo 101-0051, Japan

First published 2021 by Kinseido Publishing Co., Ltd.

Cover design	sein
Text design	Yasuharu Yuki
Video filming	Scott Berlin, Soon Jeong Chang, Charly El Hayek, Jack Sargent
Video production	Scott Berlin
Photos	Scott Berlin and Soon Jeong Chang
Text	Scott Berlin, Megumi Kobayashi
Japanese annotations	Megumi Kobayashi

Authors and publisher are grateful to everyone who appeared on the
videos.

 音声ファイル無料ダウンロード

http://www.kinsei-do.co.jp/download/4134

この教科書で DL 00 の表示がある箇所の音声は、上記 URL または QR コードにて
無料でダウンロードできます。自習用音声としてご活用ください。

▶ PC からのダウンロードをお勧めします。スマートフォンなどでダウンロードされる場合は、
ダウンロード前に「**解凍アプリ**」を**インストール**してください。

▶ URL は、**検索ボックスではなくアドレスバー (URL 表示欄)** に入力してください。

▶ お使いのネットワーク環境によっては、ダウンロードできない場合があります。

CD 00　左記の表示がある箇所の音声は、教室用 CD（Class Audio CD）に収録されています。

Introduction

After three and a half years of dedicated work this second textbook in the *World Adventures* series is presented to you. This textbook follows the same format as *World Adventures* but takes students even farther across the globe from Argentina to the Arctic Circle and from the Great Barrier Reef to the Great Wall of China. I offer my warm welcome to you and I am very happy that you are … *On Board for More World Adventures*.

It's true that today's technology can do some amazing things including translating documents from one language to another or providing detailed information on places on the other side of the world. However, technology cannot replace the most wonderful experience of interacting, talking, and sharing with people in different countries. English is the essential component for these face-to-face encounters. To put it simply, having the ability to read and speak English, even at a very basic level, will give you a much broader scope of opportunities in the world.

Creating the videos for *On Board for More World Adventures* has been the most interesting and most difficult part of this project. For each country I have selected topics and themes that I believe Japanese students would find interesting, motivating, and useful. These are not pre-scripted scenarios or constructed dialogs like you may find in many ESL videos. These are real facts, information, and experiences about each country's history, culture and trends, all shot on location. It can be quite challenging especially in cases like when trying to film fish in Australia, camels in Kuwait, and giraffes in Kenya.

Cover to cover my wife, Soon Jeong Chang, and I took the photos and made the videos for you. Doing all this during the breaks from my university made for a demanding schedule. Fortunately, once again Megumi Kobayashi sensei is the co-author. Megumi's skill and expertise has been indispensable for adding information and ideas as well as helping to write the chapters. All of us have worked very hard and I truly believe the results are a compelling synergy of multimedia, information and writing.

With my sincerest regards for all learners, use *On Board for More World Adventures* and learn from it, enjoy it, and share it.

Scott Berlin

は じ め に

今日の社会では、インターネットなどを通じて世界の情報をいち早く、映像とともに入手できるようになりました。またバーチャルな交流も、ますます広がっています。インターネットのおかげで、このように世界はずいぶんと身近になったはずです。とはいうものの、私たちはいったい他国について、どのくらい知っているのでしょうか。他国のことについて私たちが持っている知識も、そして他国のことを学ぶ機会も、実際は意外と少ないというのが現状ではないでしょうか。その上、インターネットに海外の各種情報が溢れているといっても、その多くは英語で提供されています。一般的に英語のサイトは学習者の多くにとってハードルが高く、容易には踏み込めない領域でしょう。

そんな中で *On Board for More World Adventures* は、興味をそそる世界の国々の特色をわかりやすく紹介し、現地の人々の生の声を収録した貴重な映像を提供しています。本書は他の目的で制作された映像を二次利用している教材とは異なり、最初から日本人大学生を対象として、豊富な経験を持つ著者が実際に世界各地に出向いて作成したものです。テーマ、トピック、そして使われている英語、エクササイズも日本人大学生向けに配慮されているので、身近なようで身近でない世界に、英語で臆することなく踏み込んでいけると思います。

また本書のもう一つの特色は、地元の人のインタビューを通して、世界で使用されている様々な英語——World Englishes と呼ばれています——にも出会えることです。カジュアルなインタビューは海外ニュースとは異なり、一般の人々の日常について知る絶好の機会でもあります。本書の映像からも明らかなように、世界各地でノンネイティブ・スピーカーが英語を使ってコミュニケーションを図っています。英語を使う能力があれば、世界における機会が大きく広がるということは紛れもない事実です。各地の英語の特色についても日本語で解説されていますので、世界の人々が話す生の英語に触れ、その多様性と柔軟性にぜひ目を向けてみてください。今後世界の人々と英語でコミュニケーションを図る際に、きっと大きな手助けとなると信じています。

なお本書の作成に当たって撮影にご協力いただいた皆さん、陰になり日向になり本書の作成を支えてくれた家族、そして忍耐強く細やかにサポートしてくださった金星堂編集部の皆様に心からお礼を申し上げます。

そして最後に、本書を通して学生の皆さんが英語力を伸ばし、バーチャルな世界だけでなく、実際に世界の人々と交流し、世界や自国に対する理解を深めていってくださることを願ってやみません。

小林　めぐみ

本書の使い方

最初の **Warm-up Exercise** では、各国に関する背景知識をクラスメートと一緒に活性化していきます。その国について既に何か知っていることが重要なのではなく、クイズ感覚で質問に答え、どのような国なのか想像を膨らませてください。

その後の **Vocabulary Exercise** では、続く **Reading** の中に出てくる重要単語とその意味を、マッチング形式のエクササイズで予習します。英単語の和訳ではなく英語による定義に慣れるよいチャンスでもあります。

250 〜 300 語程度の **Reading** は、これから映像を通して訪れる国々の情報をさらに増やし、内容理解を助けるために設けられています。**Reading Comprehension** で正しく理解できたか確かめてください。

映像は、2つのパートに分かれています。**Part I** は、各国についての興味深い歴史・文化・社会などを視覚的に紹介してくれます。**Vocabulary Preview** で、単語の予習をしてから映像を見てください。**First Viewing** では、写真付きの多選択肢問題形式でまず内容の大意をつかんでもらうのがねらいです。**Second Viewing** では、もう一度映像を見て、より細かな内容を問う問題に答えてください。大意から細部まで、必要ならば映像を繰り返し見て、少しずつ全体的な理解を深めていってください。

Part II は、地元の人がそれぞれの国、英語事情、自分たちの生活について話してくれるインタビュー形式となっています。教科書には各国の言語・英語事情、各スピーカーのバックグラウンド、そして彼らの英語の主な特徴が日本語で解説されており、文化的・言語的に理解を深めることができるはずです。映像を見た後は、**Check Your Understanding** で内容を確認しましょう。

最後の **On Your Own** では、各章を総括する話し合いのトピックが提供されています。各国で扱ったトピック・テーマから、日本そして自分の状況を振り返り、自分がどう思ったかクラスメートと話す（もしくは書いてまとめる）などして発信力を高めてください。

On Board for More
World Adventures

Table of Contents

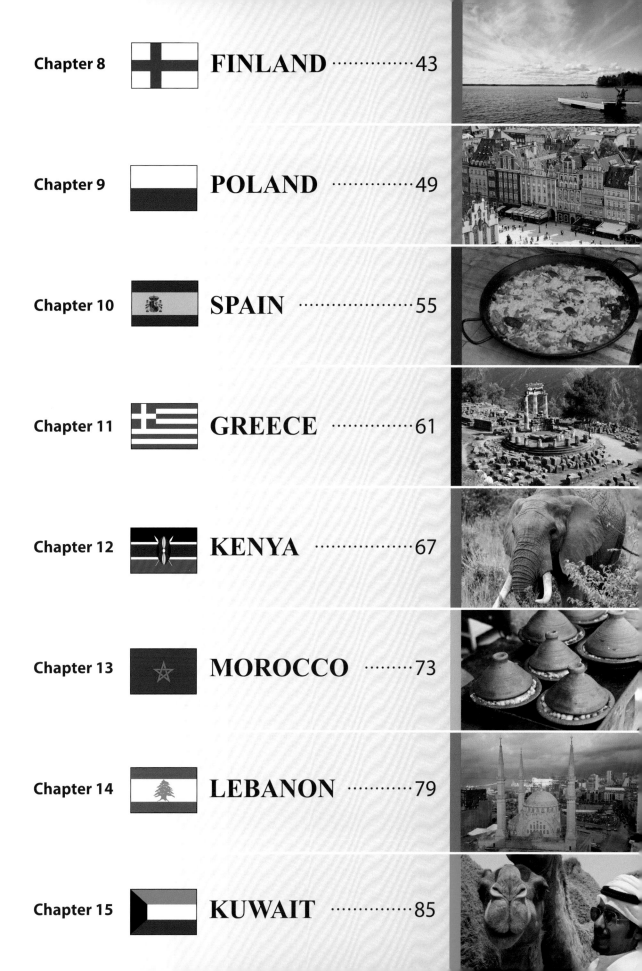

Population: 22.5 million
Size: 7,741,220 km²
Capital: Canberra ☆
Currency: Australian Dollar

Chapter 1

AUSTRALIA

南半球に位置する国オーストラリア。コアラやカンガルーなどの動物から、のどかな自然というイメージがありますが、水不足などの問題も抱えています。この章では、オーストラリアの地理や自然について理解を深めてください。

🌐 Warm-up Exercise

Complete the following exercise before continuing with the chapter.
この章の内容に入る前に、以下について考えてみましょう。

1. The first European settlement on Australia was for _____.
   a. prisoners   **b.** the King of Austria
   c. exporting kangaroo meat   **d.** trading slaves

2. Australia is the _____ largest country in the world.
   a. 5th   **b.** 6th   **c.** 7th   **d.** 8th

3. Doolboong, Kalkatungu, and Wangkumara are extinct Australian _____.
   a. tropical fish   **b.** wild kangaroos
   c. Aboriginal languages   **d.** hummingbirds

4. For five minutes, share as much as you know about Australia with your partner.

 **Vocabulary Exercise**

The following words appear in the Reading. Match the correct definition to each word.
次の単語は Reading で使われています。それぞれの単語の意味を a～e から選びなさい。

1. species （　　）　**a.** to prevent waste, decay, or loss of something

2. metabolism （　　）　**b.** the environment in which an animal or plant normally

3. conserve （　　）　　　 lives or grows

4. legend （　　）　**c.** a popular story handed down from earlier times whose

5. habitat （　　）　　　 truth has not been proven or verified

　　　　　　　　　　d. the chemical process that occurs in living organisms by

　　　　　　　　　　　which material is used to produce energy

　　　　　　　　　　e. a class or category of animals or plants having some

　　　　　　　　　　　common characteristics or qualities

 **Reading**　　　　　　　　　　　　　　　　　　　DL 02　　CD 02

Koala

　　Everyone knows the adorable symbol of Australia, the koala bear. However, the koala is not a bear at all; it is a marsupial. A marsupial is a mammal, and the most distinguishing feature is that the females have a pouch for feeding and raising their babies. Koalas weigh from 9 to 30 pounds with the southern Australia **species** of koalas being larger and heavier. Koalas eat
5　eucalyptus leaves and almost nothing else. Eucalyptus leaves have little nutrition, so koalas digest very slowly and have a slow **metabolism** to **conserve** energy. That is why you rarely see koalas moving fast. They also sleep for up to 18 hours a day to save energy. They usually don't drink water because they get all the necessary water from the eucalyptus leaves.

　　Koalas have played an important part in Australia's history. For many centuries the
10　Aborigines have passed on myths and **legends** about koalas. In fact, the word koala is believed to originate from one Aboriginal dialect meaning "no drink." In the early 1900's, koalas were hunted almost to extinction for their soft fur, causing the Australian government to list koalas as a "Protected Species." Unfortunately, once again, koalas are a threatened species because of **habitat** loss due to urban expansion.

15　　Koalas have some very unique features. For example, they have fingerprints like humans. On their front paws they have five digits, or fingers. Two digits face opposite the other three like our thumb. This helps the koalas grasp tree branches as they climb. The most surprising thing is the sound
20　they make. Koalas make a nasty, deep, and loud growl when communicating; something you would never expect to hear from the charming little icon of Australia.

Notes

eucalyptus「ユーカリ」　Aborigine「アボリジニ（オーストラリアの先住民族）」　growl「唸り声」

🌐 Reading Comprehension

Complete the following exercise.
Reading の内容と合うように 1 〜 5 の空欄に英語を書き入れなさい。

1. Female marsupials have a _____ for feeding and carrying their babies.
2. Koalas need to save their energy because the eucalyptus leaves have _____ _____.
3. Because of its _____ _____ the koala was hunted almost to extinction.
4. The special fingers that koalas have help them to _____ _____ _____.
5. What surprised the author about koalas?

_____

Part I GETTING TO KNOW AUSTRALIA online/video

🌐 Vocabulary Preview 🎧 DL 03 💿 CD 03

Before watching the video, study the vocabulary below.
映像に出てくる語彙を確認しておきましょう。

1. hemisphere　　半球
2. constellation　星座
3. equator　　　　赤道
4. arid　　　　　　乾燥地帯の
5. outback　　　　オーストラリアの内陸の田舎、奥地
6. beak　　　　　　くちばし
7. Uluru National Park
　　ウルル（＝カタ・ジュタ）国立公園（オーストラリア大陸中央部に位置し、ウルルまたは Ayers Rock と呼ばれる一枚岩で有名）
8. aquifer　　　　帯水層（地下水を多く含む地層）
9. replenish　　　補給する、再び満たす
10. Great Barrier Reef
　　グレートバリアリーフ（オーストラリア北東部沿岸に続く大サンゴ礁）
11. coral reef　　　サンゴ礁

Answer the following questions based on the video.
映像を見て、以下の問いに答えなさい。

1. Which of the following is true about Australia's geography?
   a. It is called "down under" because the temperature is low in Australia.
   b. The Southern Cross is the name of the Australian national flag.
   c. It is a dry continent, and part of the land is desert.
   d. Australia is the second smallest continent.

2. Using water from aquifers for a city's water supply creates a problem because ...
   a. it only rains 20 to 25 cm per year.
   b. the water is very deep in the ground.
   c. the water is not replenished.
   d. they use one meter of water per year.

3. Which is true about Uluru?
   a. It is 10,000 years old.
   b. It is part of the most popular tour package in Australia.
   c. The Aborigines created some of the cracks in the rock.
   d. A large part of the rock is hidden beneath the ground.

4. Which is NOT true about the Great Barrier Reef?
   a. It is visible from space.
   b. It is made from lots of small reefs.
   c. Scuba diving is the only way you can see it.
   d. We need to protect it so it will not be destroyed.

 **Second Viewing** *Focusing on the details*

Watch the video again and choose the correct answer.
もう一度映像を見て、（　　）内の適切な言葉を選びなさい。

1. The Southern Cross is a constellation that can only be seen south of the (equator / Ecuador).

2. Australia is the second driest continent after (an arctic area / Antarctica).

3. Seventy percent of the land in Australia is (desert / arid or semi-arid).

4. Scott thinks that the (great cities are / outback is) the biggest attraction in Australia.

5. The birds with the orange beak are useful if you are lost because they will help you to (find water / become rescued).

6. The average rainfall in the (central / coastal) area is 20 to 25 cm per year.

7. To the Aborigines, Uluru is a (secret / sacred) place.

8. The Great Barrier Reef has 1,500 different kinds of (fish / coral).

 Part II

▶ ENGLISH IN AUSTRALIA　　online / video

オーストラリアの人口は約 2300 万人ですが、そのうち 4 分の 1 ほどが国外で生まれた移民からなる多民族国家です。英語が事実上の公用語ですが、移民家庭では様々な言語が使用され、教育機関では英語以外の言語の学習が推奨されています。オーストラリアの英語は、イギリスの容認英語（Received Pronunciation）とロンドンの下町ことばであるコックニーに近い発音（例えば every day が every die のように聞こえる発音）が多く受け継がれています。G'day, mate（あいさつのことば）、Good on ya（いいね）、No worries（心配しないで、どういたしまして）などはフレンドリーでオーストラリアらしい表現と考えられています。また barbie, breakie, arvo, journo といった独自の短縮語が多く使われているのが特徴です（それぞれ barbeque, breakfast, afternoon, journalist）。

 Personal Interview

Read about James before you watch the interview of him.
ジェームズさんについて以下の情報を読み、インタビューを見ましょう。

Speaker Profile

Name	James
Age	26
Hometown	Blacktown
Family	Single

 James' English ここに注意！
G'day で始まるあいさつなど、オーストラリア英語らしい特徴が満載です。take が若干「タイク」に近い発音になっていることに注意してください。他にも part, worst, culture など、母音のあとの /r/ 音が発音されないのもイギリス標準英語と同じです。

Check Your Understanding

Watch the video and do the following exercise.
映像を見て、以下の問いに答えなさい。

1. What area of Australia does James work in?
   a. The whole country
   b. Central Australia
   c. Near the Great Barrier Reef

2. What does James say about language barriers?
   a. He doesn't like meeting people who speak little English.
   b. He enjoys language barriers as an important cultural experience.
   c. Language barriers make it difficult to communicate important messages.

3. Which of the following does James NOT mention as one of the best parts of Australia?
   a. The geography is beautiful.
   b. The crime rate is low.
   c. The traveling is easy.

4. What does James say about his future dream?
   a. He has a lot of future dreams.
   b. He wants to keep learning about Australia and the world.
   c. He wants to travel around the world himself.

On Your Own

Discuss the following questions with your partner.
あなたもパートナーと話し合ってみましょう。

1. What are some things you could do in your daily routine to save water?
2. What do you think is the (long-term) impact on the environment from buying bottled water like Evian and Volvic?

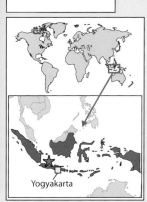

Yogyakarta

Population: 253.6 million
Size: 1,904,569 km²
Capital: Jakarta ⭐
Currency: Indonesian Rupiah

Chapter 2
INDONESIA

バリ島で有名なインドネシアは多数の島々からなる南国の多民族国家。この章では都会の喧騒と伝統的な影絵芝居やボロブドゥール寺院などの建築物から、多彩な文化が息づくこの国の魅力を感じ取ってください。

🌐 Warm-up Exercise

Complete the following exercise before continuing with the chapter.
この章の内容に入る前に、以下について考えてみましょう。

1. Before 1945, Indonesia was under _____ colonial rule.
    a. Dutch   **b.** Portuguese   **c.** German   **d.** Spanish

2. Which of the following does Indonesia have the most of?
    a. Climate zones   **b.** Cultures   **c.** Languages   **d.** Active volcanoes

3. Which animal is native only to the islands of Sumatra and Borneo?
    a. Otter civet   **b.** Orangutan   **c.** Vampire bat   **d.** Pelican

4. For five minutes, share as much as you
   know about Indonesia with your partner.

The following words appear in the Reading. Match the correct definition to each word.
次の単語は Reading で使われています。それぞれの単語の意味を a ～ e から選びなさい。

1. excavate ( ) **a.** returning something to a former or original condition
2. ascend ( ) **b.** to move, climb, or go upward
3. neglect ( ) **c.** to expose or unearth by digging
4. looted ( ) **d.** taken by pillaging, dishonesty, or force
5. restoration ( ) **e.** disregard, lack of care or attention

 **Reading**

 DL 04 CD 04

Forgotten in the Jungle

Although Indonesia had been colonized by the Dutch since the 17th century, for five years beginning in 1811, Indonesia was under British administrative rule. Sir Thomas Stamford Raffles, known as the Father of Singapore, was the Lieutenant Governor in Indonesia at that time. Raffles had an interest in Javanese art and architecture. He had heard local stories about
5 an ancient monument buried in the jungle in Central Java. In 1814, Raffles sent Dutch engineer H. C. Cornelius to find the lost treasure. Mr. Cornelius found it, and after weeks of **excavating** centuries of volcanic ash and jungle growth, Borobudur was rediscovered.

There are no written records but archeologists have determined that Borobudur was built between the 8th and 9th centuries during the Sailendra Dynasty. It was built as a Buddhist
10 temple but presents a unique blend of Indian Gupta art and Javanese Buddhist architecture. Borobudur is 34.5 meters high and 123 meters on each side, making it the largest Buddhist temple in the world. Visually it is spectacular. There are nine terraces, and as you **ascend**, each terrace represents a higher level of enlightenment. From above, it looks like a giant Buddhist Mandala.

15 Although it is not clear why Borobudur was abandoned, many believe it was because the main religion of Indonesia changed to Islam. Then slowly from **neglect**, volcanoes, and jungle, the temple vanished. Ironically, being buried actually protected it. Once rediscovered, the new challenge was to preserve this world heritage. Originally there were 504 statues of the Buddha, however, 43 of them have been **looted** as souvenirs.

20 The biggest threat to Borobudur has been nature itself. Rain, pollution, and fungus rapidly erode the volcanic stones. The UNESCO organization did a **restoration** project costing over 20 million dollars from 1975 to 1982. Today Borobudur is Indonesia's number one tourist attraction.

Notes

Sir Thomas Stamford Raffles「サー・トマス・スタムフォド・ラッフルズ（1781-1826、イギリスの植民地建設者）」 Lieutenant Governor「副総督」 Borobudur「ボロブドゥール遺跡」 Sailendra Dynasty「シャイレーンドラ朝（8 ～9世紀半ばにかけてジャワ島中部に建てられた仏教王朝）」 Gupta art「インドのグプタ朝（320~600 頃）の古代インド最盛期の美術」 Mandala「曼荼羅（仏教の世界観を表現した絵画など）」

🌐 Reading Comprehension

Complete the following exercise.
Reading の内容と合うように 1 〜 5 の空欄に英語を書き入れなさい。

1. Why did Sir Raffles send Mr. Cornelius to find the hidden monument?

   _____

2. Why are the exact dates of the construction of Borobudur not known?

   _____

3. The terraces represent the different _____ _____ _____.

4. Today, there are a total of _____ remaining Buddhist statues at Borobudur.

5. _____ _____ and _____ are causing damage to the stones.

Part I

GETTING TO KNOW INDONESIA   online / video

🌐 Vocabulary Preview

 DL 05   CD 05

Before watching the video, study the vocabulary below.
映像に出てくる語彙を確認しておきましょう。

1.	National Monument	国家独立記念塔（ジャカルタの公園「ムルデカ広場」にあり、モナスと呼ばれる）
2.	epic tale	叙事詩、壮大な物語
3.	puppet	操り人形 （なお puppeteer は操り人形師、人形遣い）
4.	relief carving	レリーフ、彫刻
5.	*Ramayana*	「ラーマーヤナ」（古代インドの叙事詩）
6.	triumph	勝利する、打ち負かす
7.	UNESCO Masterpiece of the Oral and Intangible Heritage of Humanity	
		ユネスコ人類の口承及び無形遺産の傑作

Answer the following questions based on the video.

映像を見て、以下の問いに答えなさい。

1. Which is NOT true about Indonesia's geography?
   a. Because of the soil and weather, spices grow well.
   b. It is located between the Pacific and Chinese Oceans.
   c. There are many volcanoes.
   d. Indonesia is in a good location for trade.

2. Which is true about Indonesia's religion?
   a. Each island has a different belief.
   b. Hindu religion has recently been introduced.
   c. The majority of Indonesians believe in Islam.
   d. Buddhism had the strongest impact.

3. What is Wayang Kulit?
   a. Indonesia's shadow puppets
   b. The name for a master puppeteer
   c. An old story of good overcoming evil
   d. The name of a Hindu state in Indonesia

4. What did Scott NOT learn about the puppets from Mr. Eddy?
   a. The character of some of the puppets
   b. How difficult it is to tell a good story
   c. How long it takes to make a puppet
   d. How hard it is to hold and move the puppets

 **Second Viewing** *Focusing on the details*

Watch the video again and choose the correct answer.
もう一度映像を見て、（　　）内の適切な言葉を選びなさい。

1. With all the noise and (pollution / population), Jakarta can be a shock.
2. Volcanoes have helped create rich (soil / oil) in Indonesia.
3. There are thousands of (languages / islands) in Indonesia.
4. Two classic shadow puppet stories are from the (Hindu / Buddhist) religion.
5. At Borobudur, religious teachings are shown in (carvings / writings).
6. The main theme in *Ramayana* is (man-vs-woman / good-vs-evil).
7. Scott thinks (seeing Mr. Eddy's / trying his own) puppet performance was a treat.
8. It takes a week to make one shadow puppet because it is (so small / hand-made).

Part II ▶ **ENGLISH IN INDONESIA** online/video

> インドネシアは多数の島からなり、ジャワ語、スンダ語、バリ語など、何百もの言語が存在します。インドネシアは植民地として長い間オランダの支配を受けていましたが、オランダ語話者はごくわずかで、国内の共通語にはマレー語を基とするインドネシア語が公用語として定められました。一方今日では英語習得熱のため授業を英語で行う学校も急増し、国語としてのインドネシア語の維持が懸念されています。インドネシア語話者の英語の発音の特徴は、/r/ 音が比較的強く発音されること、/f/ と /p/ の音を混同したりすること（例えば film が pilm になる）などが挙げられます。また語末の /ch/ 音が /ts/ になる(例えば watch が wats となる)傾向があります。

 Personal Interview

Read about Anggara Sri Wisnu before you watch the interview of him.
アンガラさんについて以下の情報を読み、インタビューを見ましょう。

Speaker Profile

Name	Anggara Sri Wisnu
Age	32
Hometown	Yogyakarta
Family	Single

 Anggara's English ここに注意！
アンガラさんは全体的に落ち着いた口調で話していますが、インドネシアの地名は早口に聞こえます。**Sri, th**r**ee** などの /r/ 音が強く発音され、**think** が **thing** のように聞こえるのが特徴です。なお途中 **Javanese** が出てきますが、**Japanese** と間違えないように。

Check Your Understanding

Watch the video and do the following exercise.
映像を見て、以下の問いに答えなさい。

1. What does Anggara's first name mean in English?
   a. Tuesday
   b. King
   c. Indian god

2. What does Anggara want to do in his future?
   a. Be a master puppeteer like his father
   b. Be a traditional dancer
   c. Be a businessman

3. What is in Anggara's favorite Javanese soup?
   a. Meat and vegetables
   b. Chicken and tofu
   c. Spices and beef

4. What is one reason Anggara might enjoy his current job as a traditional dancer?
   a. He is traditional.
   b. It's also his hobby.
   c. It's an interesting part of Indonesian culture.

On Your Own

Discuss the following questions with your partner.
あなたもパートナーと話し合ってみましょう。

1. Tell an old traditional Japanese story (myth or folktale) to your partner.
2. What kind of story (love story, fairy tales, non-fiction, etc.) interests you most? Why?

12

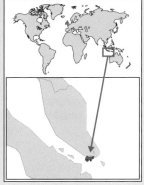

Population: 5.56 million
Size: 697 km^2
Currency: Singapore Dollar

Chapter 3

SINGAPORE

シンガポールは、ガーデン・シティーとも呼ばれ、都市計画によって国土が整備されています。
この章では、シンガポールのシンボル、マーライオンや国の成り立ちについて学ぶとともに、
シンガポールがどのように国土を美しく保っているのか見てみましょう。

🌐 Warm-up Exercise

Complete the following exercise before continuing with the chapter.
この章の内容に入る前に、以下について考えてみましょう。

1. What is the meaning of the name Singapore?
   - **a.** The Lion City
   - **b.** Siamese Forest
   - **c.** China's Port
   - **d.** The Singing Fisherman

2. Which of the following would you NOT be fined for in Singapore?
   - **a.** Not flushing the public toilet
   - **b.** Feeding the birds in public
   - **c.** Eating on public transportation
   - **d.** Wearing sandals in public buildings

3. Where does the largest number of tourists to Singapore come from?
   - **a.** Malaysia
   - **b.** Australia
   - **c.** Indonesia
   - **d.** India

4. For five minutes, share as much as you know about Singapore with your partner.

The following words appear in the Reading. Match the correct definition to each word.
次の単語は Reading で使われています。それぞれの単語の意味を a ～ e から選びなさい。

1. hand-in-hand (　　) **a.** to be equal or at the same level
2. parallel (　　) **b.** to disappear, go away, especially quickly
3. vanish (　　) **c.** to form an idea or notion of something
4. curator (　　) **d.** a person in charge of a museum, art collection, etc.
5. conceive (　　) **e.** indicating that two things are related or normally go together

 **Reading**　　　　　　　　　　　　　　　　 DL 06　CD 06

The Merlion

Any conversation about Singapore surely will go **hand-in-hand** with a mention of the Merlion. The Merlion has achieved symbolic recognition that **parallels** other world icons, such as the Eiffel Tower, the Statue of Liberty, and Big Ben. Unlike those icons, Singapore's Merlion is a mythical creature that originates from the combination of a story about a prince and a desire
5　to create a tourist souvenir.

Prince Sang Nila Utama "founded" Singapore in the 14th century. The story goes: one day the prince was hunting on the Malay Peninsula when he saw a deer. He chased the deer up a hill. The deer **vanished**, but from the hilltop the prince could see an island he had never seen before. He sailed there and when he arrived on the island he saw a powerful and fierce creature
10　he had never seen before. When he asked what animal it was, he was told it was a *singa*: the Sanskrit word for lion in the local dialect. The prince decided to rename the small fishing village on the island to *Singapura*: lion city.

In 1964, Alec Fraser-Brunner was the **curator** of the aquarium in Singapore. He **conceived** the logo of a fish with the head of a
15　lion. The lion head surely reflects back on the story of Prince Utama and the founding of Singapore. As for the body of a fish, Brunner did work at the aquarium. Another possible connection to the fish is that Singapore was originally a small fishing village. Or Brunner could have known about ancient Etruscan coins which have the
20　image of a Merlion on them. Whatever his inspiration was, we are grateful, because today the Merlion is the symbol of Singapore around the world.

Notes

Merlion「マーライオン（シンガポールの象徴的存在）」 Prince Sang Nila Utama「シュリーヴィジャヤ王国の王子サン・ニラ・ウタマ」 The story goes「話はこうだ」 Etruscan「エトルリア（人）の（前8世紀頃からイタリア中央部にいた民族）」

 **Reading Comprehension**

Complete the following exercise.

Reading の内容と合うように 1 〜 5 の空欄に英語を書き入れなさい。

1. The Merlion, the Statue of Liberty, and Big Ben are recognized as _____
   _____.

2. What animal did the prince see when he was on the Malay Peninsula?
   _____

3. What language is the word *singa* from? _____

4. Where did Brunner work in 1964? _____

5. Where did the image of a Merlion first appear?
   _____

Part I

 GETTING TO KNOW SINGAPORE online video

 Vocabulary Preview  🎧 DL 07 ◎ CD 07

Before watching the video, study the vocabulary below.
映像に出てくる語彙を確認しておきましょう。

1.	city-state	都市国家
2.	litter	ゴミ（特に公共の場に捨てられたゴミ。littering はゴミのポイ捨てを指す）
3.	fine	罰金
4.	component	要素、成分
5.	Sir Thomas Stamford Raffles	サー・トマス・スタムフォド・ラッフルズ（近代シンガポールの創設者）
6.	East India Trading Company	東インド会社
7.	sprawling	不規則に伸びる、だらしなく広がる
8.	Jackson Plan	ジャクソン・プラン（シンガポールの都市計画の一つ）
9.	Green Plan	グリーン・プラン（シンガポールの都市計画の一つ）
10.	compromise	（安全性などを）危険にさらす、損なう
11.	sustainability	持続可能性
12.	Island of Sentosa	セントーサ島（シンガポールの人気リゾート）

NO RIDING
FINE : $ 1000

Answer the following questions based on the video.
映像を見て、以下の問いに答えなさい。

1. Scott is impressed by Singapore because…
   a. even the Merlion is being cleaned up.
   b. it is one of the three city-states in the world.
   c. it is clean despite the high population density.
   d. there are many tourist spots and parks.

2. Which is NOT mentioned as the reason Singapore is so clean?
   a. There are fines for inappropriate behaviors.
   b. The government hires many workers to clean the city.
   c. There are many signs that tell people what is not allowed.
   d. People actually follow rules in Singapore.

3. Which is true about city planning in Singapore?
   a. Sir Raffles designed the city himself 200 years ago.
   b. Despite the Jackson Plan, the city grew into a large mess.
   c. Various plans have been introduced and updated since the 19th century.
   d. The Green Plan in 1992 was mainly concerned with the need of the present generation.

4. Which is true about the Merlion statues?
   a. There are about five of them around the city.
   b. All of them are gushing water from the mouth.
   c. The one on Sentosa Island is the original.
   d. The smallest Merlion is behind city hall.

 **Second Viewing** *Focus on the details*

Watch the video again and choose the correct answer.
もう一度映像を見て、（　　）内の適切な言葉を選びなさい。

1. Scott feels an obligation to show the Merlion because it is (celebrating its 40th birthday / Singapore's icon).

2. People joke about Singapore as a "(fine / funny)" city.

3. Fines are (just one / the most effective) method of Singapore's city plan.

4. Sir Raffles established (a trading post / the East India Trading Company).

5. The Jackson Plan was introduced in (1819 / 1822).

6. The goal of (sustainability / economic development) was added to the Green Plan in 2006.

7. Singaporeans feel that (lawmakers / they) are responsible for their environment.

8. Scott seems to be (impressed / disappointed) with the small Merlion.

 Part II

ENGLISH IN SINGAPORE

online / video

東西貿易の拠点として古くから繁栄してきたシンガポールでは、公用語も英語、マレー語、中国語（北京語）、タミル語の4つが採用されています。住民の多くは中国系ですが、ビジネス、行政の場では英語が主流です。ただし日常使われるシンガポールの英語は、各民族の母語から影響を受けた Singlish と呼ばれる方言。主語を省略して Can と答える、強調のために Can can! と繰り返す、Can lah（できるよ）のように語尾に語気助詞をつける、過去についても現在形のまま使用する、マレー語（makan 食べる、jalan-jalan 散歩する）や中国語の単語が取り入れられているなどの特徴があります。音声面では、語末の子音が頻繁に脱落する（例えば car park がカッパーと聞こえる）のが顕著な例です。

 Personal Interview

Read about "CS" before you watch the interview of her.
シーエスさんについて以下の情報を読み、インタビューを見ましょう。

Speaker Profile

Name	Lim Cai Shi (nickname: "CS")
Age	32
Hometown	Singapore
Family	Single

 CS's English ここに注意！
シーエスさんの発音では、**th**ree が tree となったり、語尾の子音が脱落する例が見られます。favorite や chicken rice の発音に注意して聞いてみてください。

Watch the video and do the following exercise.

映像を見て、以下の問いに答えなさい。

1. What does CS indicate about English in Singapore?
    a. Singapore's English education system is effective.
    b. Special schools begin teaching English at the age of three or four.
    c. It is the language of communication among many races.

2. What does CS NOT say about the Chinese New Year?
    a. It is the biggest holiday in Singapore.
    b. Fireworks are one of the New Year's favorite events.
    c. People gather to celebrate the government.

3. What does CS mention about both Singapore and Japan?
    a. They are clean.
    b. They have low crime rates.
    c. They need more relaxation places.

4. What is true about CS?
    a. She has an older brother.
    b. She wants to help dogs.
    c. She thinks her best friend is very smart.

On Your Own

Discuss the following questions with your partner.

あなたもパートナーと話し合ってみましょう。

1. What do you think are the pros and cons of having many fines like Singapore?
2. Do you have some family rules at home (curfew, chores, etc.)? Do you follow them and what is the punishment if you don't follow the rules? Do you think the punishment is fair?

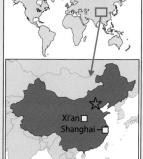

Population: 1.35 billion
Size: 9,596,960 km²
Capital: Beijing ☆
Currency: Chinese Yuan

Chapter 4

CHINA

長い歴史を持つ中国。この章では始皇帝の墓陵、万里の長城、紫禁城といった世界遺産から上海にそびえたつ高層ビルまで、壮大なスケールと独特の雰囲気をもった中国の建造物を通して中国の歴史に触れてみましょう。

🌐 Warm-up Exercise

Complete the following exercise before continuing with the chapter.
この章の内容に入る前に、以下について考えてみましょう。

1. China is known for having the longest _____ in the world.
   a. river　　**b.** dynasty　　**c.** highway　　**d.** sea bridge

2. What is believed to be the most likely origin of the name "China"?
   a. Qin, the name of the first emperor and dynasty
   b. Xien, the Mongolian word for the Han people
   c. Cina, the Sanskrit word for Middle Kingdom
   d. Shina, a mispronunciation of a word meaning "original people"

3. Which of the following was NOT invented by the Chinese?
   a. Gunpowder　　**b.** Sundial (used to tell time)
   c. Toilet paper　　**d.** Compass

4. For five minutes, share as much as you know about China with your partner.

 **Vocabulary Exercise**

The following words appear in the Reading. Match the correct definition to each word.
次の単語は Reading で使われています。それぞれの単語の意味をa〜eから選びなさい。

1. ambitious   (   )   **a.** to begin, start in motion, or originate
2. initiate   (   )   **b.** to dig or get out of the earth, uncover
3. unearth   (   )   **c.** to gather or bring together, put or fit together
4. unimaginable (   )   **d.** difficult or impossible to believe
5. assemble   (   )   **e.** showing eagerness, desire to obtain wealth, power, or achieve a goal

 **Reading**    DL 08   CD 08

Terracotta Warriors

Long before the movie *The Bucket List* came out, I made a list of goals I wanted to achieve. One goal was to see the Terracotta Warriors of China. Not long ago my wife Soon Jeong and I were on a trip through China. I made sure our schedule included a stop in Xi'an to see the Terracotta Warriors.

5   The first emperor of China, Qin Shi Huang, was an **ambitious** builder. He **initiated** the construction of the first parts of the Great Wall of China and he also built his own mausoleum and tomb. About 1.5 km from his tomb, he had an entire army made of clay placed in the ground. These 8,000 plus soldiers are the Terracotta Warriors and their purpose was to protect the emperor in his afterlife.

10   The Terracotta Warriors were discovered by some local farmers in 1974. The farmers were digging a well when they **unearthed** the top of one warrior. Today there are three pits that have been uncovered revealing the army, including foot soldiers, generals, archers, horses, and carriages. The discovery has been called the greatest archeological discovery of the 20th century.

15   When we went there, I was really fascinated by the fact that each figure is life-size and has its own unique face. No two figures are exactly the same. I stared at them and could actually feel the expressions in their faces. I was also amazed at the **unimaginable** task of putting the warriors back together. When 20 they were uncovered, the thousands of figures were broken into pieces. I was told by our guide that only one figure known as The Archer was found completely intact. Still today archeologists are **assembling** the broken figures.

Notes

The Bucket List「『最高の人生の見つけ方』（2007年のアメリカ映画。ここでは死ぬ前にやりたいことのリストを意味する）」 Terracotta Warriors「兵馬俑」 Xi'an「西安」 Qin Shi Huang「秦の始皇帝（259BC-210BC）」 Great Wall of China「万里の長城」 mausoleum「霊廟」 well「井戸」 pit「採掘場」

Reading Comprehension

Complete the following exercise.
Reading の内容と合うように 1 〜 5 の空欄に英語を書き入れなさい。

1. Scott made his list of goals _____ the movie *The Bucket List* was made.
2. The Terracotta Warriors were made to _____ the emperor after he died.
3. _____ discovered the clay soldiers by accident in 1974 when they were digging a _____.
4. Each figure has a unique face and is _____.
5. The Archer was the only Terracotta Warrior found that was not _____.

Part I

GETTING TO KNOW CHINA

 online video

Vocabulary Preview

🎧 DL 09 ◎ CD 09

Before watching the video, study the vocabulary below.
映像に出てくる語彙を確認しておきましょう。

1. millet　　　雑穀類（キビ、ヒエ、アワなど）
2. Qin Dynasty　　　秦王朝
3. rammed earth　　　版築（土や石、石灰などの混合物で土壁や建築の基礎部分を堅固にする）
4. Ming Dynasty　　　明王朝
5. complex　　　建物などの集合体
6. Forbidden City　　　紫禁城
7. symmetry　　　左右対称、調和美
8. Qing Dynasty　　　清王朝
9. Oriental Pearl TV Tower　　　東方明珠電視塔（上海テレビ塔）
10. Shanghai World Financial Center　　　上海環球金融中心（上海ワールドフィナンシャルセンター）
11. Shanghai Tower　　　上海中心（上海タワー）

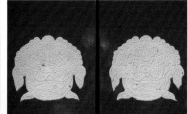

Answer the following questions based on the video.
映像を見て、以下の問いに答えなさい。

1. What is the main focus or theme of the video?
   a. Chinese historical buildings
   b. The amazing things the Chinese have built
   c. Some of the achievements of Chinese emperors
   d. Revealing how much the Chinese love achieving world records

2. The Great Wall of China…
   a. was made of bricks during the Qin Dynasty.
   b. is one long wall, 5,000 miles long.
   c. was completed by the first emperor of China.
   d. is several walls that took centuries to complete.

3. What could be said about the emperor's new home built in 1406?
   a. It was big enough to be a city.
   b. Common people were ordered to maintain the buildings.
   c. The architectural style was modern and creative.
   d. Nine hundred families lived there.

4. At the time of the video, what could you say about China's tall buildings?
   a. China is slowing down and building fewer tall buildings.
   b. China has the ten tallest buildings in the world.
   c. China has more of the ten tallest buildings than any other country.
   d. The Oriental Pearl TV Tower is the 4th tallest building in the world.

 **Second Viewing** | *Focus on the details*

Watch the video again and choose the correct answer.
もう一度映像を見て、（　　）内の適切な言葉を選びなさい。

1. The first emperor of China started to build the Great Wall in (10,000 / 221) BCE.

2. The Great Wall was built to (defend against enemies / create jobs for the economy).

3. The Great Wall built during the (Ming / Qin) Dynasty was made of wood and rammed earth.

4. Construction of the Forbidden City was completed in (1406 / 1420).

5. An even number of columns and centered doors is an example of (symmetry / wealth).

6. The Forbidden City has yellow roof tiles because (other colors are forbidden / it is the imperial color).

7. The (Shanghai / Pearl TV) Tower will be 140 meters taller than the World Financial Center.

8. Scott thinks the Chinese will build (more / fewer) tall buildings in the future.

Part II ENGLISH IN CHINA

(online / video)

中国語は母語話者人口が世界第 1 位で、英語をしのぐ世界言語ですが、英語は中国社会において社会的、経済的成功に直結する武器として習得熱が高まっています。2001 年には小学校での英語が必修化されており、大学では College English Test（大学英語考試）で最低 4 級（英検 2 級程度に相当）を取得することが卒業要件になっています。中国語話者の英語は、一般に母音の長短が曖昧になる（sheep/ship が同じになる）、語末の有声子音が無声化もしくは脱落する（cab が cap, ca になる）、また一部の方言では /n/ と /l/ が混同する（night と light が同じになる）例などが見られます。

 Personal Interview

Read about "Rinjo" before you watch the interview of her.
リンジョーさんについて以下の情報を読み、インタビューを見ましょう。

Speaker Profile

Name	Wu Xiaoyu (nickname: "Rinjo")
Age	20
Hometown	Shandong Province
Family	Single

 Rinjo's English ここに注意！

リンジョーさんの英語は、living が leaving に聞こえるなど、母音の長さが曖昧になったり、通常 in my opinion となるところが for my opini(on) となったりしています。very という単語もウェリーに近い音になっているので注意して聞いてみましょう。

Check Your Understanding

Watch the video and do the following exercise.
映像を見て、以下の問いに答えなさい。

1. Rinjo says being able to communicate with foreigners is one advantage of…
   a. living in Beijing.
   b. speaking English.
   c. traveling to Tibet.

2. Which of the following descriptions matches Rinjo's image of Japan?
   a. A polite Japanese person reading manga and eating sashimi
   b. A busy Japanese person reading manga and eating sushi
   c. A polite Japanese person reading manga and eating bento

3. Why does Rinjo want to go to Tibet?
   a. Because it is in China.
   b. Because she wants to meet more foreigners.
   c. Because it is very beautiful.

4. What does Rinjo think about English grammar compared to Chinese grammar?
   a. English grammar is similar and very difficult.
   b. English grammar is very different and difficult.
   c. English grammar is different and not difficult.

On Your Own

Discuss the following questions with your partner.
あなたもパートナーと話し合ってみましょう。

1. What would be on your bucket list? (You must list at least five goals.)
2. What are the most famous monuments or buildings in Japan? Why are they famous?

Iguazu Falls

Population: 42.6 million
Size: 2,780,400 km²
Capital: Buenos Aires ★
Currency: Argentine Peso

Chapter 5

ARGENTINA

アルゼンチンと言えばタンゴで有名ですが、私たちの想像以上にアルゼンチンの人々にとってタンゴは身近な日常生活の一部のようです。その華麗な動きを目で楽しんでください。迫力のあるイグアスの滝も絶景です。

🌐 Warm-up Exercise

Complete the following exercise before continuing with the chapter.
この章の内容に入る前に、以下について考えてみましょう。

1. Which of the following is Buenos Aires often called?
   - **a.** Little Athens
   - **b.** The Manhattan of the South
   - **c.** The Paris of South America
   - **d.** Spanish Beijing

2. Argentina is NOT one of the top-five world producers of _____.
   - **a.** tea
   - **b.** soybeans
   - **c.** sunflower
   - **d.** lemon

3. What is the national sport of Argentina?
   - **a.** Soccer
   - **b.** Pato
   - **c.** Baseball
   - **d.** Volleyball

4. For five minutes, share as much as you know about Argentina with your partner.

The following words appear in the Reading. Match the correct definition to each word.
次の単語は Reading で使われています。それぞれの単語の意味を a〜e から選びなさい。

1. steeped （　　） **a.** to make a loud sucking noise when eating or drinking

2. presence （　　） **b.** to remove by rubbing with a cloth, paper, or hand

3. wipe off （　　） **c.** soaked in water or other liquid to bring out flavors

4. slurp （　　） **d.** the existence of someone or something in a particular place

5. generate （　　） **e.** to bring into existence, cause to be produced or created

 **Reading**   DL 10  CD 10

Drinking Argentina's Culture

Morning coffee is pretty much a standard around the world, although in Argentina you are likely to see people drinking *mate* instead. *Mate* (mah-tay) is a drink made of ground-up leaves from the *Yerba mate* tree and **steeped** in hot water. Drinking *mate* goes back centuries to the native Guarani people of the region. Their legend explains that a Guarani man helped the moon

5 goddess, Yari, so she gave him the *Yerba mate* plant to make the "Drink of Friendship." *Mate* is the official national drink of Argentina and an average of 5 kilograms per year is consumed for each person in Argentina.

The *Yerba mate* tree is a relative of the holly plant, which is full of health benefits. *Mate* contains 24 vitamins and minerals including vitamin A, E, C, B1, B2, calcium, magnesium, and

10 many antioxidants. Because of its high nutrition, Argentine *gauchos* live on little more than meat and *mate*. They call *mate* "a liquid vegetable." However, recently there are concerns about the **presence** of Polycyclic Aromatic Hydrocarbons (PAHs) in *mate*, which are known to cause cancer. The likely source of PAHs is from the fire roasting of the leaves when processing.

15 In Argentina *mate* is a deep part of the culture. Friends will share a cup of *mate* drinking from the same straw called a *bombill*a. It is rude to **wipe off** the straw when offered a drink. Also, you should not **slurp** too much when the liquid is gone. In Buenos Aires you can often see several friends sharing one cup

20 of *mate* together. It is said that a cup of *mate* **generates** small communities between those who share it and helps construct bridges between cultures. This green drink is visible everywhere in Argentina; even Starbucks offers a *mate* flavored latte.

Notes

ground-up < 原形 grind「すりつぶした」　*Yerba mate*「イェルバ（もしくはジェルバ）・マテ」　Guarani「グアラニー族（南米の先住民族）」　holly「セイヨウヒイラギ」　antioxidant「抗酸化剤、酸化防止剤」　*gaucho*「ガウチョ（南米のカウボーイ。スペイン人と先住民の混血住民を指すことが多い）」　Polycyclic Aromatic Hydrocarbons (PAHs)「多環芳香族炭化水素」　*bombilla*「ボンビーリャ（マテ茶用ストロー）」

 **Reading Comprehension**

Complete the following exercise.
Reading の内容と合うように 1 ～ 5 の空欄に英語を書き入れなさい。

1. According to the legend, how did the Guarani people get the *Yerba mate* tree?

   _____

2. Which plant is the *Yerba mate* tree a relative of? _____

3. What do the Argentine *gauchos* call *mate*? _____

4. When friends share a drink of *mate*, what should they NOT do?

   _____

5. When people share a cup of *mate*, what do they say it creates?

   _____

Part I   **GETTING TO KNOW ARGENTINA** online / video

Vocabulary Preview　　　　　　DL 11　　CD 11

Before watching the video, study the vocabulary below.
映像に出てくる語彙を確認しておきましょう。

1. La Boca　　　　　ラ・ボカ（首都ブエノスアイレスの地区）
2. competition　　　競技会、コンペ
3. *milonga*　　　　ミロンガ（アルゼンチンタンゴを踊る場所）
4. inspire　　　　　（感情を）引き起こす、その気にさせる
5. improvisation　　即興
6. Iguazu National Park　　イグアス国立公園

Answer the following questions based on the video.
映像を見て、以下の問いに答えなさい。

1. Which is true about tango dance in Argentina?
   a. It has a long history and is a deep part of the culture.
   b. It is pop culture and a recent trend in dancing.
   c. You need to go to special clubs to see tango.
   d. It originated in Spain.

2. Which is true about learning to dance tango?
   a. Tango schools are open all night.
   b. You must be slim and flexible in order to dance tango.
   c. Schools teach you to follow all the steps exactly in order.
   d. There are many different moves and a few basic steps.

3. Iguazu Falls has received the title of…
   a. Second Largest Falls of Argentina.
   b. Best National Park since 1934.
   c. Largest Water Fall System of South America.
   d. New Seven Wonders of Nature.

4. In Iguazu National Park, what do the walkways allow you to do?
   a. Walk under the falls
   b. Get close to the falls at different levels
   c. Cross the river to the Brazil side
   d. See all 275 falls in the waterfall system

Second Viewing *Focus on the details*

Watch the video again and choose the correct answer.
もう一度映像を見て、（　　　）内の適切な言葉を選びなさい。

1. Tango was created in the (19th century / 20th century).
2. Tango (clubs / dancers) are called *milongas*.
3. Tango schools teach the different (moves / music) that can be used.
4. Learning tango is mostly about the (correction / connection) between partners.
5. The size of Argentina ranks as number (one / two) in South America.
6. At Iguazu, most of the falls are on the (Argentine / Brazilian) side of the river.
7. Over (14 / 4) thousand gallons of water go over Iguazu Falls every second.
8. If you take the boat to see Iguazu Falls, you are guaranteed to get (wet / close).

Part II

ENGLISH IN ARGENTINA   online / video

アルゼンチンの公用語はスペイン語ですが、イタリア系移民が多く、イタリア語の影響を強く受けた独特なスペイン語方言が発達したと言われています。また国民の多くがヨーロッパ系移民で、ヨーロッパ志向が強いとも言われています。英語教育に関しては、フォークランド紛争（マルビナス戦争）などからイギリスへの政治的反発がある一方、世界の共通語としての英語は小学校から導入するなどして積極的に受け入れ、南米では英語が最も浸透している国と報告されています。（スペイン語話者の一般的な英語の音声の特徴については、スペインの章参照。）ただし、アルゼンチンのスペイン語では1人称の yo（通常ヨ、ジョ）がショと発音されたり、動詞 esta がエスタではなく、エッタになったりします。このような特徴が英語の発音にも現れる可能性があるでしょう。

 Personal Interview

Read about Paula before you watch the interview of her.
パウラさんについて以下の情報を読み、インタビューを見ましょう。

Speaker Profile

Name	Paula
Age	34
Hometown	Buenos Aires
Family	Single

 Paula's English ここに注意！

パウラさんは英語を日常的に使用する仕事柄かクセのない英語を話していますが、文末のイントネーションに注意してみてください。ほぼ上昇調になっています。

 **Check Your Understanding**

Watch the video and do the following exercise.
映像を見て、以下の問いに答えなさい。

1. Why is Paula's favorite color green?
   a. Because she is wearing a green jacket.
   b. Because it goes well with her hair.
   c. Because it is the national color.

2. What does Paula think of Japan?
   a. She admires Japan because they are the hardest workers in the world.
   b. She admires Japan but feels sorry that Japan has so many crises.
   c. She admires Japan because they can recover from any crises.

3. What did Paula study when she went to the university?
   a. English
   b. Tango singing
   c. Translation

4. What does Paula say about the attraction to tango dance?
   a. It is difficult to explain, but once you start you cannot stop dancing it.
   b. Dancing in the *milongas* is a great way to find a boyfriend or girlfriend.
   c. People are addicted to tango because of the music and tango singers.

On Your Own

Discuss the following questions with your partner.
あなたもパートナーと話し合ってみましょう。

1. What kind of dance would you like to learn and why?
2. What do you think is Japan's national passion? Is it your passion too?

Population: 118 million
Size: 1,964,375 km²
Capital: Mexico City ☆
Currency: Mexican Peso

Chapter 6

MEXICO

タコスやサルサといったメキシコの食文化は日本でもおなじみですが、他にも世界中で愛されている食べ物でメキシコ原産のものがあります。それは何でしょうか。また、メキシコに残る遺跡からメソアメリカの古代文明についても学びましょう。

🌐 Warm-up Exercise

Complete the following exercise before continuing with the chapter.
この章の内容に入る前に、以下について考えてみましょう。

1. Which day do Mexican children traditionally receive gifts?
   a. Halloween, Oct. 31   **b.** Christmas, Dec. 25
   c. New Year's Day, Jan. 1   **d.** Three Kings Day, Jan. 6

2. What is the name of the city in Mexico that is famous for cliff diving?
   a. Mazatlán   **b.** Cancún   **c.** Acapulco   **d.** Puerto Vallarta

3. How many states does Mexico have?
   a. 31   **b.** 41
   c. 51   **d.** 61

4. For five minutes, share as much as you
   know about Mexico with your partner.

 **Vocabulary Exercise**

The following words appear in the Reading. Match the correct definition to each word.
次の単語は Reading で使われています。それぞれの単語の意味を a〜e から選びなさい。

1. delectable （　　） **a.** having or seeming to have the power to do miracles
2. cultivate （　　） **b.** a feeling of being tired, lack of energy
3. serpent （　　） **c.** enjoyable, highly appealing, appetizing food
4. miraculous （　　） **d.** a snake
5. fatigue （　　） **e.** to prepare and work on (land) to grow crops

 **Reading**  DL 12 CD 12

Theobroma

In Greek *Theos* means God, and *Broma* means food, so *Theobroma* translates to "Food of the gods." Many of us might agree with this translation because *Theobroma Cacao* is used to make the **delectable** treat, chocolate. The history of cacao goes back thousands of years.

Evidence clearly shows that between 1500-400 BCE the Olmec Indians of Mesoamerica
5 made a drink from cacao, and it is believed that they also **cultivated** the plant. For the Maya, cacao was an important part of their society and economy. The Maya believed that *Kakaw* was given to them by the feathered **serpent**, Kukulkan. Later when Christopher Columbus saw natives with cacao seeds, he only noted the seeds were used as money. In 1521 when the Spanish entered Tenochtitlan, they were offered a cacao drink by the Aztec ruler, Moctezuma
10 II. The Spanish introduced the bitter cacao drink to Europe. Sometime in the 1500's, Europeans began adding cane sugar to the drink and this greatly increased the demand for cacao. Before long, the French had cacao plantations in the Caribbean. In 1847, the first chocolate bar was invented. Milk chocolate was created by Daniel Peter in 1875 in Switzerland. In 1879, he and Henri Nestlé started the Nestlé Co.
15 The Belgian chocolate maker Godiva opened in 1926. Today, 3 million tons of cacao is produced annually making it a 100 billion dollar per year industry.

Cacao and various products made with it have been said to do **miraculous** things. It has been claimed to cure **fatigue**,
20 improve digestion, stimulate the nervous system, cure a weak heart and liver, and to be an aphrodisiac. We now know that cacao has flavonoids which are known to have health benefits. It might not be the food of the gods, but it sure is heavenly.

Notes

Olmec Indians of Mesoamerica「メソアメリカ文明の母体となったオルメカ人」 Kukulkan「ククルカン（羽を持つ蛇の姿をしたマヤ神話の創造神）」 Tenochtitlan「テノチティトラン（アステカ帝国の首都）」 Moctezuma II「モクテスマ 2 世（c.1466-1520、アステカ帝国第 9 代の君主）」 aphrodisiac「催淫薬、媚薬」 flavonoid「フラボノイド（有機化合物。ポリフェノールの一種。抗酸化作用があると言われる）」

🌐 Reading Comprehension

Complete the following exercise.
Reading の内容と合うように 1 ～ 5 の空欄に英語を書き入れなさい。

1. What are the earliest years that we know cacao was being used? _____

2. What is the Maya name for the feathered serpent? _____

3. What did Christopher Columbus think cacao seeds were used for?

   _____

4. Who was the ruler of Tenochtitlan? _____

5. Which company was first, Godiva or Nestlé? _____

Part I ▶ GETTING TO KNOW MEXICO   online / video

🌐 Vocabulary Preview
🎧 DL 13   💿 CD 13

Before watching the video, study the vocabulary below.
映像に出てくる語彙を確認しておきましょう。

1.	Zocalo	ソカロ（メキシコシティの中心広場）
2.	Chichén Itzá	チチェン・イッツァ遺跡
3.	Palenque	パレンケ遺跡
4.	Kabah	カバー（カバフ）遺跡
5.	contribution	貢献
6.	Temple of Inscriptions	碑文の神殿
7.	hieroglyph	神聖（象形）文字
8.	settlement	居住地
9.	Comalcalco	コマルカルコ遺跡
10.	pod	さや
11.	pulp	繊維（質）
12.	fermented	発酵させた
13.	milled	粉砕された

Answer the following questions based on the video.
映像を見て、以下の問いに答えなさい。

1. Which is NOT true about the large plaza Scott is standing in?
   - **a.** It is called Zocalo.
   - **b.** It is the center of Mexico.
   - **c.** It is the same location as the capital of the Aztec Empire.
   - **d.** It was much bigger 500 years ago.

2. What could be said about Chichen Itza?
   - **a.** It was built in the postcolonial period of Maya history.
   - **b.** It only lasted a couple of centuries.
   - **c.** It is where the Pyramid of Kukulkan is located.
   - **d.** It is the most famous icon of Mexico.

3. Which is true about Palenque?
   - **a.** Palenque was discovered in the early 1970's.
   - **b.** Researchers accidentally broke part of the Temple of Inscriptions.
   - **c.** The hieroglyphs told the history of Palenque's rulers.
   - **d.** At Palenque, the Maya people gave important contributions to their rulers.

4. Which is NOT true about cacao?
   - **a.** Fermenting removes the pulp from the seeds.
   - **b.** Only the rich and powerful could have this drink in Maya society.
   - **c.** The Maya sometimes used it as money.
   - **d.** The thin shell is mixed in to enhance the flavor.

 **Second Viewing** *Focusing on the details*

Watch the video again and choose the correct answer.
もう一度映像を見て、（　　）内の適切な言葉を選びなさい。

1. (Zocalo / Tenochtitlan) was the name of the Aztec capital city.
2. The (Maya / Aztec) Indians had more impact on Mexico.
3. The number of steps on the Pyramid of Kukulkan probably represents the (days in a year / number of rulers of Chichen Itza).
4. Researchers decoded the Maya writing in the (Temple of Inscriptions / Pyramid of Kukulkan).
5. The Maya formed (a unified empire / small settlements) across the Yucatan Peninsula.
6. Oyster shells at Comalcalco show how the Maya (utilized local resources / fished).
7. Cacao is known to be a (native / national) plant of Mexico.
8. In order to make a chocolate liquor, the seeds are finally (milled / roasted).

 Part II **ENGLISH IN MEXICO** online / video

メキシコには 60 以上の先住民言語が存在すると言われていますが、国民の９割以上がスペイン語を話し、事実上の公用語となっています。隣国アメリカ合衆国は一番の貿易相手国であり、交流も盛んなため、メキシコのスペイン語には多くの英語が流入しています。（逆にメキシコ系住民の多いアメリカの地域では、スペイン語に影響を受けた Chicano English と呼ばれる方言も発達しています。）スペイン語話者の英語の特徴はスペインの章で詳しく説明しますが、メキシコでは、/y/ を /j/ と発音する（例えば yesterday が jesterday となる）のが特徴です。

 Personal Interview

Read about Jesus before you watch the interview of him.
ヘスースさんについて以下の情報を読み、インタビューを見ましょう。

Speaker Profile

Name	Jesus Hau
Age	32
Hometown	Merida
Family	Married

 Jesus' English ここに注意！
英語では umm や hmm などをつなぎ言葉としてよく使いますが、ヘスースさんは日本語の「えーと」に近い eh… を使っています。また probably の強勢が弱い（標準的には第一音節に強勢）、learn が若干ルーンのように聞こえるなどの特徴があります。

Watch the video and do the following exercise.
映像を見て、以下の問いに答えなさい。

1. Jesus says learning about the different cultures is the most _____ part of his job.
   a. difficult
   b. enjoyable
   c. helpful

2. Jesus wants to open a _____ in the future.
   a. Maya village
   b. youth hostel
   c. Maya bakery

3. Which of the following did Jesus NOT mention about Japan?
   a. He wants to visit Kyoto.
   b. He likes the history.
   c. He likes the food.

4. Jesus' wife was taking _____ lessons when he met her.
   a. English
   b. Japanese
   c. Spanish

🌐 **On Your Own**

Discuss the following questions with your partner.
あなたもパートナーと話し合ってみましょう。

1. Tell what you would put in a Japan village theme park.
2. Name the brand of chocolate you think is the best. And how often do you eat it?

Wurzburg Rothenburg
Mannheim
 Castle Route
 Nuremberg
Romantic Munich
Route Fussen

Population: 80.9 million
Size: 357,022 km²
Capital: Berlin ☆
Currency: Euro

Chapter 7

GERMANY

ビールとソーセージで有名なドイツですが、グリム童話のイメージそのままの古城も多くの観光客を魅了してやまないドイツの財産です。ライン川クルーズや観光街道沿いの古城の情景は、中世ヨーロッパの雰囲気たっぷりです。

🌐 Warm-up Exercise

Complete the following exercise before continuing with the chapter.
この章の内容に入る前に、以下について考えてみましょう。

1. How many UNESCO World Heritage sites are there in Germany?
    a. 9 **b.** 19 **c.** 39 **d.** 59

2. Which is the most popular castle in Germany?
    a. Burg Eltz **b.** Heidelberg **c.** Burg Hohenzollern **d.** Neuschwanstein

3. Regarding beer consumption, Germany ranks _____ in the world.
    a. 1st **b.** 2nd
    c. 3rd **d.** 4th

4. For five minutes, share as much as you
    know about Germany with your partner.

The following words appear in the Reading. Match the correct definition to each word.
次の単語は Reading で使われています。それぞれの単語の意味を a ～ e から選びなさい。

1. commemorate ( ) **a.** to formally sanction or give official power
2. prolong ( ) **b.** unsuitable, not sufficient, not meeting standards
3. patron ( ) **c.** to extend the duration, lengthen in the time
4. inadequate ( ) **d.** to serve as a memorial or reminder
5. authorize ( ) **e.** a person who is a customer, client, or paying guest

Reading  DL 14　CD 14

Festival with the Wrong Name

Carnival in Rio de Janeiro, Mardi Gras in New Orleans, and Sapporo's Snow Festival are all famous international celebrations. However, the biggest festival in the world is Oktoberfest in Munich, Germany. Surprisingly, most of Oktoberfest is not held in October.

On October 12, 1810, Prince Ludwig (who later became King Ludwig I) married Princess

5　Therese. To **commemorate** their wedding they threw a big party. All the citizens of Munich were invited to enjoy music, food, and drink. Five days later the celebration ended with some horse races that the royal family attended. It was so much fun they did it again the next year, and the year after that, and after that. Soon it became an annual event and in a short time Oktoberfest expanded. In 1811 an agriculture show was added, 1818 had the first carousel, and in the 1870's

10　mechanical rides appeared. The festival was **prolonged** to 16 days and moved up to September to take advantage of the warmer weather. Nowadays, Oktoberfest ends on the first Sunday of October.

Today, over six million **patrons** from all over the world come to Oktoberfest and drink between six and a half to seven million liters of

15　beer. Just any beer would be **inadequate**; it must be official Oktoberfest beer that is brewed within the city limits of Munich. There are only six breweries that are **authorized** to produce Oktoberfest beer. In addition, these breweries must strictly follow the German Beer Purity Law of 1487 to have their beer served in the many beer tents at Oktoberfest.

20　The biggest celebration in the world also includes a parade, ferris wheel, roller coaster, magicians, entertainers, and lots of food and music of all kinds. Prost!

Notes

Mardi Gras「マルディグラ（ルイジアナ州ニューオリンズの謝肉祭、カーニバル）」 Oktoberfest「オクトーバーフェスト（ドイツ・バイエルン州の最大の都市ミュンヘン (Munich) で催される世界最大の祭り）」 Prince Ludwig「バイエルン王太子 (1786-1868、のちのルートヴィヒ 1 世)」 Princess Therese「テレーゼ王女 (1792-1854、ルートヴィヒの妃)」 carousel「回転木馬」 brewery「ビールの醸造所」 German Beer Purity Law「ビール純粋令（ビールの原料を限定するもの。1516 年の純粋令では、水、麦芽、ホップ、酵母のみとしている。)」 ferris wheel「観覧車」 Prost「『プロースト』ドイツ語で乾杯の意」

Reading Comprehension

Complete the following exercise.
Reading の内容と合うように 1 〜 5 の空欄に英語を書き入れなさい。

1. In 1810, Prince Ludwig and Princess Therese threw a big party to _____
   _____ _____.

2. Who was invited to the celebration? _____

3. How long did the first Oktoberfest last? _____

4. Why was Oktoberfest moved to September?
   _____

5. Only six breweries are allowed to _____ _____ _____.

Part I GETTING TO KNOW GERMANY online/video

Vocabulary Preview 🎧 DL 15 ◎ CD 15

Before watching the video, study the vocabulary below.
映像に出てくる語彙を確認しておきましょう。

1.	Rhine River	ライン川
2.	Rothenburg	ローテンブルク
3.	Romantic Route	ロマンチック街道（Romantic Road と呼ばれることも。ドイツ語では Romantische Straße）
4.	boost	後押しする、高める
5.	Würzburg	ヴュルツブルク
6.	medieval	中世の
7.	Füssen	フュッセン
8.	Neuschwanstein Castle	ノイシュヴァンシュタイン城
9.	King Ludwig II of Bavaria	バイエルン王ルートヴィヒ2世
10.	retreat	閑居、静養先、別荘
11.	Castle Route	古城街道（Castle Road。ドイツ語で Burgenstraße）
12.	monastery	修道院
13.	Nuremberg	ニュルンベルク

Getting the main idea

Answer the following questions based on the video.
映像を見て、以下の問いに答えなさい。

1. Which is true about the Rhine River?
    a. It has recently been used for transportation.
    b. There is only one three-hour cruise offered.
    c. Tourists only use it for convenient transportation.
    d. Many tourists enjoy the river cruises.

2. Which is NOT true about the Romantic Route?
    a. You can travel by bicycle along the route.
    b. There are many medieval cities along the route.
    c. It goes from Rothenburg in the north to Füssen in the south.
    d. It was created to help the local economy.

3. Which is NOT true about Neuschwanstein Castle?
    a. It is located near Füssen.
    b. It is the main attraction on the Castle Route.
    c. It was built by the King of Bavaria.
    d. It is one of the most famous castles in the world.

4. Scott thinks drinking some German beer is…
    a. a journey.
    b. a part of German culture you should try.
    c. a must-do at every destination.
    d. better when it's made by small breweries.

Second Viewing *Focusing on the details*

Watch the video again and choose the correct answer.
もう一度映像を見て、（　　）内の適切な言葉を選びなさい。

1. On a Rhine River cruise, there is much to (see / do).
2. (Würzburg / Rothenburg) is surrounded by an old wall.
3. There are (21 / 28) towns along the Romantic Route.
4. King Ludwig II slept in Neuschwanstein castle (many / a few) times.
5. The best way to enjoy the Castle Route is to (rent a car / use a travel agent).
6. Both the Romantic Route and Castle Route were (created in the 1950's / famous from medieval times).
7. The Castle Route runs from (north to south / east to west).
8. Many German beer manufacturers are (global / local) breweries.

Part II ENGLISH IN GERMANY   online / video

ドイツの公用語はドイツ語ですが、ドイツには様々な民族がおり、近年はトルコからの移民をはじめとして、さらに多様化が進んでいます。ドイツの英語教育は州によって異なりますが、小学校低学年から指導が始まります。ドイツ語と英語は同じゲルマン語であり、文法や語彙などに共通点が多々あります。例えばドイツ語の Haus、Mutter は英語の house、mother ですし、ドイツ語話者にとって英語は比較的習得しやすい言語と言えるでしょう。音声に関しては、ドイツ語では、例えば <u>V</u>olkwagen（フォルクスヴァーゲン）のように /v/ の音が /f/ と発音されたり、Dachshun<u>d</u>（ダックスフント）のように語末の子音が無声化（/d/ → /t/）したりするので、ドイツ語話者の英語にもこのような特徴が見られる場合があります。またドイツ語では sp と st の /s/ が /ʃ/ と発音されるので、<u>s</u>port や <u>s</u>tudent がシュポート、シュトゥーデントとなる可能性があります。

 Personal Interview

Read about Michael before you watch the interview of him.
マイケルさんについて以下の情報を読み、インタビューを見ましょう。

Speaker Profile

Name	Michael Buchheim
Age	30
Hometown	Landsberg am Lech
Family	Married

 Michael's English ここに注意！
マイケルさんの英語ではインフォーマルな表現 cuz (because) や wanna (want to) が使われています。また **with** がやや **wiz** のように聞こえます。

⊕ Check Your Understanding

Watch the video and do the following exercise.
映像を見て、以下の問いに答えなさい。

1. What does Michael say about the landscape in Bavaria?
    a. It is big.
    b. It is perfect.
    c. It is very relaxing.

2. Why would Michael want to meet one of the bad people in the world?
    a. To understand why and how they can do bad things
    b. To learn how to do bad things to people
    c. To teach them why bad things shouldn't be done

3. Why does Michael say there is nothing difficult about his job?
    a. Because his wife and friends help him.
    b. Because he only serves breakfast and does check in and check out.
    c. Because he is happy from his soul.

4. What does Michael say about being healthy, happy, and helping people?
    a. These are the benefits he gets from his job.
    b. It is what he wants to achieve.
    c. It is his secret for success.

⊕ On Your Own

Discuss the following questions with your partner.
あなたもパートナーと話し合ってみましょう。

1. Tell your partner about the best journey you have experienced.
2. Tell your partner about the festival you want to attend most and why.

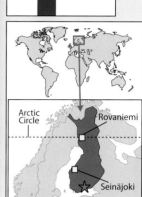

Population: 5.26 million
Size: 338,145 km²
Capital: Helsinki ☆
Currency: Euro

Chapter 8

FINLAND

フィンランドはスウェーデンとロシアに挟まれた北欧の小国ですが、**IT** 産業が盛んで、携帯電話メーカーのノキアの国として有名です。また教育大国としても世界的な注目を浴びています。この章ではムーミンやフィンランドの機能的なデザインに着目してみましょう。

🌐 Warm-up Exercise

Complete the following exercise before continuing with the chapter.
この章の内容に入る前に、以下について考えてみましょう。

1. Pesäpallo is the national sport of Finland and it is very similar to _____.
   a. baseball   **b.** soccer   **c.** ice hockey   **d.** bowling

2. Which of the following is a Finnish brand?
   a. Red Bull   **b.** H&M   **c.** IKEA   **d.** Arabia

3. Which of the following is NOT an annual contest held in Finland?
   a. Wife Carrying contest
   b. Mobile Phone Throwing Championship
   c. Reindeer Riding contest
   d. Air Guitar World Championship

4. For five minutes, share as much as you know about Finland with your partner.

The following words appear in the Reading. Match the correct definition to each word.
次の単語は Reading で使われています。それぞれの単語の意味をa〜eから選びなさい。

1. fictional ( )   **a.** to be broadcasted or televised
2. inspire ( )   **b.** a short trip or outing to someplace
3. excursion ( )   **c.** to decorate or add to make more attractive
4. aired ( )   **d.** to motivate, affect, or produce a feeling or idea
5. adorn ( )   **e.** imaginary, unreal

 **Reading**

 DL 16   CD 16

Moomin

In 1945 Tove Jansson wrote a children's book titled *The Moomins and the Great Flood*. It was the first of nine books she would write about the Moomins: a family of cute hippo-like characters known as Moomintroll, Moominmamma and Moominpappa, and their friends.

The Moomins are not purely **fictional** characters. They are somewhat based on the author's
5 own family, life, and experiences. The word Moomin came from Tove's uncle who said that if she tried to sneak food from the kitchen, the Moomintroll, who lived in the closet, would breathe cold air down her neck. Moominmamma was based on Jansson's own mother and Too-Ticky, the dear friend of the Moomin family, was **inspired** by Tove's life-long partner, Tuulikki Pietilä.

In addition, the adventures of the Moomins often happen on or around water, which was
10 also similar to the experiences of the Jansson family. Retreating to a summer cottage as well as a sauna are national ways of relaxation for the Finns. The Janssons, too, spent their summers at their cottage on a small island enjoying swimming and boating **excursions**.

The Moomin series became so popular that in 1954 Tove
15 began writing a Moomin comic strip for a London-based newspaper. In 1990, a TV company produced Moomin cartoons that were **aired** in over 60 countries including Japan. This was the beginning of "Moomin Mania." Currently, the Moomin company has annual sales over 600 million dollars,
20 35% of which is generated in Japan. Today, the Moomin character is also actively used as a Finnish icon: the Moomins **adorn** the wings of Finnair and the mugs of Arabia.

Notes

Tove Jansson「トーベ・ヤンソン（1914-2001、ムーミン・シリーズを描いたフィンランドの画家・作家）」
Tuulikki Pietilä「トゥーリッキ・ピエティラ（1917-2009、フィンランド人グラフィック・デザイナー）」 Arabia「アラビア（フィンランドの陶器ブランド）」

Reading Comprehension

Complete the following exercise.
Reading の内容と合うように 1 〜 5 の空欄に英語を書き入れなさい。

1. The Moomin characters are based on the author's own _____,
   _____, and _____.
2. Who created the word Moomin? _____
3. Where did Ms. Jansson's family go in the summers?
   _____
4. Tove started writing a _____ _____ for a newspaper in 1954.
5. What started Moomin Mania?
   _____

Part I

GETTING TO KNOW FINLAND online video

Vocabulary Preview DL 17 CD 17

Before watching the video, study the vocabulary below.
映像に出てくる語彙を確認しておきましょう。

1. Alvar Aalto アルヴァ・アアルト（1898-1976）フィンランドの建築家、デザイナー
2. hands-on 実践的な、参加型の
3. project-based learning プロジェクト型学習
4. PISA (Programme for International Student Assessment) OECD（経済協力開発機構）の生徒の学習到達度調査
5. consistently 常に、一貫して
6. Arctic Circle 北極線（北極圏の限界線を示す北緯66度33分線。北極圏では真冬に太陽が昇らない極夜と真夏に太陽が沈まない白夜の現象が起こる。）

Answer the following questions based on the video.
映像を見て、以下の問いに答えなさい。

1. Which is true about design in Finland?
    a. It is integrated into everyday life.
    b. Finnish people think a good design will stand out in its environment.
    c. A product's design is considered more important than its function.
    d. Finnish brands are not widely known outside of Finland.

2. Which is true about education in Finland?
    a. A teacher is highly respected but their salary is less than average.
    b. Finnish students have performed well on PISA tests.
    c. The focus of Finnish education is to teach students about equality.
    d. There are no tuition fees at schools except for the universities.

3. Students in Finland generally have a lot of...
    a. tests.
    b. homework.
    c. science classes.
    d. projects.

4. Which is NOT true about Santa's village in Finland?
    a. Santa Claus "lives" there.
    b. Tourists can see Santa Claus in person if he is not busy.
    c. There is a line that indicates the Arctic Circle.
    d. You must pay a fee to cross the Arctic Circle in the village.

 **Second Viewing** *Focus on the details*

Watch the video again and choose the correct answer.
もう一度映像を見て、（　　）内の適切な言葉を選びなさい。

1. (Helsinki / Seinäjoki) was awarded for its designs in 2012.
2. Scott gives examples of Finnish design, including a (smart phone / bus stop).
3. Alvar Aalto is famous for his designs of a town hall, church, and (library / playground) in Seinäjoki.
4. According to Scott, the Finns notice design when it is (missing / integrated into the environment).
5. The Finnish education system is (different / adapted) from other countries.
6. Elementary students in Finland have more (homework / recess) than students in the US.
7. On the PISA tests, math, science, and (reading / writing) are assessed.
8. In Finnish education, (ranking students by test scores / project-based learning) is considered important.

 Part Ⅱ **ENGLISH IN FINLAND** online video

> フィンランドでは、国民の 90% がフィンランド語、5% 程度がスウェーデン語を使用
> していますが、他の北欧諸国と同じく英語も広く浸透しています。学校教育もさること
> ながら幼い頃からテレビで英米の番組に吹き替えなしで親しんでいることが英語習得に
> 役立っていると多くのフィンランドの人は感じているようです。フィンランド人の英語
> の特徴は、/s/, /ʃ/, /z/ 音の混同（Sue, shoe, zoo が同じ発音になる）、語頭にアクセン
> トが置かれる、/r/ 音が強いなどが挙げられます。

 Personal Interview

Read about Satu before you watch the interview of her.
サトゥーさんについて以下の情報を読み、インタビューを見ましょう。

Speaker Profile

Name	Satu Pekkala
Age	29
Hometown	Keminmaa
Family	Single

 Satu's English ここに注意！
聞き慣れないフィンランド語の固有名詞は、難しく感じるでしょう。また environmental
の /v/ が /w/ となって、エヌワイロンメンタルのように聞こえるので注意しましょう。

Watch the video and do the following exercise.
映像を見て、以下の問いに答えなさい。

1. Satu says…

    a. mosquitoes are the worst thing about Finland.

    b. she wants to teach civil engineering.

    c. she likes midsummer better than Christmas.

2. What does Satu say about English in Finland?

    a. People speak German better than English.

    b. Young people can speak English.

    c. Students practice English daily.

3. How does Satu stay healthy?

    a. By going to the sauna

    b. By eating well

    c. By spending time in nature

4. Which is true about Satu?

    a. She met her boyfriend in Germany.

    b. She went to Budapest for her last trip.

    c. She doesn't have a pet.

On Your Own

Discuss the following questions with your partner.
あなたもパートナーと話し合ってみましょう。

1. Of all the items and designs in the video, which did you like best and why? What was your impression of Finnish design?

2. How important is a product's design when you buy something (e.g., computer, smart phone, furniture, etc.)? What is more important for you than design (e.g., cost, functions, size, etc.)?

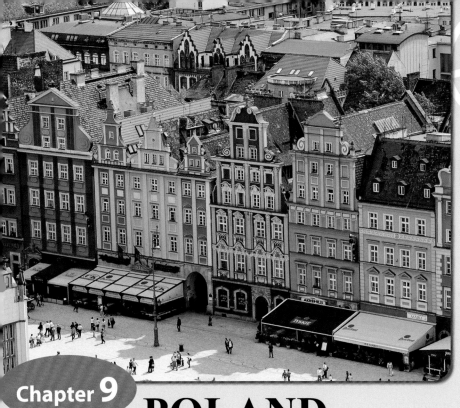

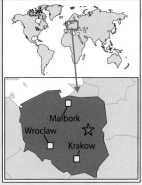

Population: 38.3 million
Size: 312,685 km²
Capital: Warsaw ⭐
Currency: Euro

Chapter 9

POLAND

この章では、ポーランドの古都を訪ねます。首都ワルシャワ以外は、ヴロツワフ、クラクフ、マルボルクなどあまり聞き慣れない都市が登場してきますが、美しい街並みを鑑賞し、ポーランドの歴史に触れてみてください。

🌐 Warm-up Exercise

Complete the following exercise before continuing with the chapter.
この章の内容に入る前に、以下について考えてみましょう。

1. The following people are all Polish EXCEPT _____.
   - **a.** Nicolaus Copernicus
   - **b.** Pope John Paul II
   - **c.** Marie Curie
   - **d.** Isaac Newton

2. Which of the following fruit is Poland the number one producer of?
   - **a.** Raspberry
   - **b.** Apple
   - **c.** Fig
   - **d.** Orange

3. Approximately how many different family names are there in Poland?
   - **a.** 100
   - **b.** 4000
   - **c.** 100,000
   - **d.** 400,000

4. For five minutes, share as much as you know about Poland with your partner.

The following words appear in the Reading. Match the correct definition to each word.
次の単語は Reading で使われています。それぞれの単語の意味を a 〜 e から選びなさい。

1. outlaw ( ) **a.** to announce or declare in an official manner
2. proclaim ( ) **b.** to make illegal
3. anonymous ( ) **c.** to prove the truth by evidence, confirm
4. anticipate ( ) **d.** to expect or consider before
5. verify ( ) **e.** without any name of author or contributor

 **Reading**  DL 18 CD 18

Unpopular Ideas

There have been many ideas in history that have changed the world. However, many of these ideas were staunchly resisted, rejected, and even **outlawed** when they first appeared. Such was the case when a Polish astronomer named Nicolaus Copernicus was able to prove that the planets revolved around the sun and not the earth. For over a thousand years, the accepted
5 scientific "fact" was that the earth was at the center and all the planets and sun circled around it. This was also written in the Bible and that made it the law. To **proclaim** anything different was heresy and could be punished by death.

In 1514, Copernicus wrote a small 40-page **anonymous** commentary that claimed he could explain the motion of the planets in a much easier and simpler way than the accepted model
10 at the time. Copernicus must have **anticipated** the dangers of writing such an idea because he only gave the manuscript to a few of his friends. For nearly 30 years after that, Copernicus worked to prove and **verify** his heliocentric model. He kept detailed records of the motion of the planets. By applying simple math,
15 geometry, and astronomy, he was able to explain his data and observations accurately.

In 1543, his life work was published in Latin as a 405-page book titled *On the Revolutions of the Heavenly Spheres*. Copernicus never knew of the revolution he had started. It
20 was said that he was on his deathbed when the first copy of his book was handed to him. He woke up, looked at the book, held it tightly to his chest, and then died.

Notes

staunchly「忠実に、断固として」 Nicolaus Copernicus「ニコラウス・コペルニクス（1473-1543、地動説を唱えたポーランド出身の天文学者、カトリック司祭）」 heresy「異端、異教」 heliocentric model「太陽中心説（地動説）」

🌐 Reading Comprehension

Complete the following exercise.
Reading の内容と合うように 1 〜 5 の空欄に英語を書き入れなさい。

1. Copernicus believed that the planets revolved around the ＿＿＿＿＿＿＿ and not the ＿＿＿＿＿＿＿.

2. For many years, the belief that the planets revolved around the earth was considered a scientific ＿＿＿＿＿＿＿.

3. Why did Copernicus give his commentary to only a few friends?

＿＿＿＿＿＿＿＿＿＿＿＿＿＿＿＿＿＿＿＿＿＿＿＿＿＿＿＿＿＿＿＿

4. Copernicus wrote his book in the ＿＿＿＿＿＿＿ language.

5. Why did Copernicus not know about the revolution he started?

＿＿＿＿＿＿＿＿＿＿＿＿＿＿＿＿＿＿＿＿＿＿＿＿＿＿＿＿＿＿＿＿

Part I

GETTING TO KNOW POLAND
online / video

🌐 Vocabulary Preview
🎧 DL 19 ⦿ CD 19

Before watching the video, study the vocabulary below.
映像に出てくる語彙を確認しておきましょう。

1. pedestrian　　歩行者用の
2. dwarf　　小人
3. Wawel Castle　　ヴァヴェル城（古都クラクフにある城）
4. Frédéric Chopin　　フレデリック・ショパン（1810-1849）音楽家
5. Malbork Castle　　マルボルク城
6. The Order of Teutonic Knights
　　ドイツ騎士団（チュートン騎士団。十字軍時代の 12 世紀後半、聖地巡礼者の保護を目的として設立された宗教的かつ軍事的組織の一つ。）
7. fortress　　要塞

Answer the following questions based on the video.
映像を見て、以下の問いに答えなさい。

1. Why does Scott say Poland's modern history is sad and tragic?
   a. Because other countries invaded and ruled Poland.
   b. Because Poland did not exist until 1989.
   c. Because Polish people were at war for 123 years.
   d. Because Poland replaced the communist government.

2. Which city is famous for dwarf statues?
   a. Wroclaw
   b. Krakow
   c. Warsaw
   d. Malbork

3. Which is NOT true about Wawel Castle?
   a. It is located in Poland's oldest city.
   b. It was built 500 years ago.
   c. It is part of a UNESCO World Heritage site.
   d. It was a home of many Poland's kings.

4. Which is true about Malbork Castle?
   a. It is the world's largest castle made of bricks.
   b. It was built by Polish royalty.
   c. It is a medieval Romanesque style fortress.
   d. It was damaged but has now been completely restored.

 **Second Viewing** *Focus on the details*

Watch the video again and choose the correct answer.
もう一度映像を見て、（　　）内の適切な言葉を選びなさい。

1. Wroclaw has a (pedestrian / historic) zone in the city center.
2. One interesting tourist activity in Wroclaw is (hiding / hunting for) dwarf statues.
3. In (Krakow / Warsaw), the "old town" is a UNESCO World Heritage site.
4. Many of Chopin's compositions are (piano solos / symphonies).
5. Chopin's body is in (France / Poland).
6. The construction of Malbork Castle (started / finished) in 1406.
7. Malbork Castle was expanded to accommodate the growing number of (Teutonic Knights / residents of Polish royalty).
8. Malbork Castle was badly damaged during (communist rule / World War II).

Part II

ENGLISH IN POLAND

online / video

> ポーランドの公用語は、国民の 97% が母語とするポーランド語。また国民の 95% がカトリック教徒で、一見「単一民族」の国家であるように思われがちですが、ポーランド人の民族的出自は様々で、実態は多様な民族の融合体です。ヨーロッパの列強の干渉により、国外に移民したポーランド人も多いですが、近年はイギリスをはじめとする EU 諸国への出稼ぎに出るケースも多く、英語を学ぶ意欲も高いようです。また伝統的にドイツとの関係が緊密で、ドイツ語学習者も多くいます。なおポーランド人の英語音声の特徴には、語尾の子音が無声化する（peas と peace が同じ発音になる）、後ろから二番目の音節にアクセントが来るなどがあります。

 Personal Interview

Read about Natalia before you watch the interview of her.
ナターリアさんについて以下の情報を読み、インタビューを見ましょう。

Speaker Profile

Name	Natalia
Age	27
Hometown	Wroclaw
Family	Single

 Natalia's English ここに注意！
ナターリアさんの発音には 14 か 40 なのか、art or か art of なのかなど、どちらが正しいのか判別が難しいところがありますが、発音だけでなく文脈にも注意を払ってみましょう。

Check Your Understanding

Watch the video and do the following exercise.
映像を見て、以下の問いに答えなさい。

1. What does Natalia do?
   a. She teaches art.
   b. She is a graphic designer.
   c. She organizes English camps.

2. Which question about English did Scott NOT ask Natalia?
   a. How she learned English
   b. How many people speak English in Poland
   c. How difficult it is for Polish people to learn English

3. Natalia was able to answer the question in concrete terms about…
   a. her image of Japan.
   b. who her favorite movie star is.
   c. who she admires.

4. What does Natalia say is the best thing about Poland?
   a. Coffee
   b. Beer
   c. Politics

On Your Own

Discuss the following questions with your partner.
あなたもパートナーと話し合ってみましょう。

1. Like the dwarf statues in a Polish city, more and more Japanese cities/towns are creating their own "mascot" (e.g., *Kumamon, Funasshi,* etc.). What effects do you think these statues or mascots have on their cities/towns?

2. What are the advantages and disadvantages of pedestrian zones? In Japan's case, imagine *hokousha-tengoku* in a major street, market place, etc.

Population: 47.7 million
Size: 505,370 km²
Capital: Madrid ★
Currency: Euro

Chapter 10

SPAIN

この章では、一日5回食事をするともいわれるスペイン人の食に焦点を当てています。古都トレドの街を眺望しながら、ある特別なパン菓子に隠された楽しい仕掛けや世界一高級なイベリコ豚のハム、そしてスペインの代表的料理を目で味わってみてください。

Warm-up Exercise

Complete the following exercise before continuing with the chapter.
この章の内容に入る前に、以下について考えてみましょう。

1. Which of the following painters was not Spanish?
   a. Pablo Picasso   **b.** Edgar Degas   **c.** Salvador Dalí   **d.** Francisco Goya

2. Escudella, Roscón, and Paella are all Spanish _____.
   a. cities   **b.** guitar players   **c.** foods   **d.** dances

3. Spain is the world's largest producer of _____.
   a. olive oil   **b.** saffron
   c. wine   **d.** tomatoes

4. For five minutes, share as much as you know about Spain with your partner.

 **Vocabulary Exercise**

The following words appear in the Reading. Match the correct definition to each word.
次の単語は Reading で使われています。それぞれの単語の意味を a〜e から選びなさい。

1. infrastructure (   )   **a.** a fair, objective, and permissive attitude towards others
2. aqueduct   (   )   **b.** commonly held opinion about someone or something
3. tolerance   (   )   **c.** to cause to adopt a different religion or political model
4. convert   (   )   **d.** the basic facilities, framework, or features of a system
5. reputation   (   )   **e.** artificial channel for bringing water from a distance

 **Reading**    DL 20   CD 20

Toledo City

Toledo is like an outdoor museum. It has walls around the city, narrow cobblestone streets, old buildings, a huge stone fortress, and a cathedral that was built in the 13th century. The Tagus River surrounds the rocky hill on three sides upon which the city is located. This makes a good spot for a city because it is easy to defend. Toledo was the capital of Spain until 1560 and
5 is most widely known as the city of three cultures.

The history of Toledo goes back over two thousand years. Toledo was already a well-established city when the Romans conquered it in 193 BCE. The Romans improved the **infrastructure** of the city by building bridges, an **aqueduct**, a theater, and more. Today, ruins of some Roman baths are still visible. In the middle of the 6th century the Visigoths ruled Toledo. The Visigoths showed
10 religious **tolerance** on the Iberian Peninsula by **converting** themselves to Christianity, and at the same time, allowing Jewish people to remain in Toledo. The Moors, who took over the city in 712 AD, introduced the Islamic religion and developed Toledo into a leading city of science, art, and culture. In 1085, King Alfonso VI invaded Toledo and made it the capital of the Kingdom of Castile. King Alfonso VI allowed the Muslims to keep their religion,
15 culture, and language. Toledo became a home for Muslims, Jews, and Christians and gave Toledo the **reputation** of a city of three cultures.

Today, when you visit Toledo you can see one of the oldest continually standing synagogues in the world, old mosques that
20 have been converted to churches, and one of the best Gothic cathedrals in Europe. People say, if you haven't seen Toledo, you haven't seen Spain.

Notes

cobblestone「道路舗装用の丸石」 Tagus River「タホ川（ポルトガル語名タージョ川、英語名テグス川」 Visigoths「西ゴート族」 Iberian Peninsula「イベリア半島（スペイン・ポルトガルを含むヨーロッパ南西の半島）」 Moors「ムーア人（北西アフリカのイスラム教徒の呼称）」 Alfonso VI「アルフォンソ 6 世 (1065-1109)」 Kingdom of Castile「カスティリア王国」

Complete the following exercise.

Reading の内容と合うように 1 ～ 5 の空欄に英語を書き入れなさい。

1. Toledo is built on a _____ _____ surrounded on three sides by the Tagus River.
2. Toledo was the _____ of Spain until 1560.
3. Ruins of _____ _____ are still visible today.
4. King Alfonso VI allowed the _____ to keep their religion.
5. The cathedral in Toledo was built in the _____ style of architecture.

Part I

GETTING TO KNOW SPAIN

online/video

Vocabulary Preview

DL 21 CD 21

Before watching the video, study the vocabulary below.
映像に出てくる語彙を確認しておきましょう。

1. Roscón (de Reyes) — ロスコン（ロスコンデレジェス。王冠の形をした菓子パン）
2. Three Kings holiday — 東方三博士の日
3. figurine — 小型の人形・像
4. delicacy — 珍味、ごちそう
5. free range — 放し飼い
6. curing — 塩漬けにすること
7. cellar — （食料・燃料・ワインなどの）地下貯蔵室
8. Paella — パエリア（またはパエーリャ、パエージャ）
9. saffron — サフラン（香辛料）
10. rosemary — ローズマリー（ハーブの一種）

Answer the following questions based on the video.
映像を見て、以下の問いに答えなさい。

1. Which two things do you think Scott would most likely recommend to someone visiting Spain?
   a. Eat Spanish food and see Toledo city.
   b. Eat Roscón and see Madrid city.
   c. Bring your friends and enjoy the architecture.
   d. Enjoy the Tomatina festival and see a bullfight.

2. Which is true about Roscón?
   a. It is eaten on New Year's Day.
   b. It was originally a king's treat.
   c. A small figurine is hidden inside.
   d. The figurine can be exchanged for money.

3. Which is NOT true about Jamón de Bellota?
   a. Only black Ibérico pigs are used.
   b. Sea salt is used to prevent bacteria.
   c. It is an expensive, special delicacy.
   d. The pigs are free range only for a few months.

4. What is the most likely reason people say "The best Paella is made in Valencia?"
   a. In Valencia, they add fresh rosemary to the Paella.
   b. In Valencia, they use pans specially made for Paella.
   c. Valencia has fresher seafood for Paella because it is next to the sea.
   d. Valencia is where Paella was first made.

Second Viewing *Focusing on the details*

Watch the video again and choose the correct answer.
もう一度映像を見て、（　　）内の適切な言葉を選びなさい。

1. The focus of the video is to introduce traditional Spanish (foods / recipes).
2. (Salvador Dalí / Gaudi) is a famous Spanish architect.
3. The person who gets the figurine in the Roscón will have to (buy dinner / pay for the Roscón).
4. Bellota means (a special kind of black Ibérico pig / acorn) in Spanish.
5. The hams must go through several curing rooms with a different temperature and (humidity / pressure).
6. The ham is placed in large (coolers / cellars) to age for up to three years.
7. To properly prepare Paella, you should cook it (in a special Paella pan / outside on a grill).
8. The final ingredient to add to Paella is (rice / rosemary).

Part II ENGLISH IN SPAIN

`online` `video`

> スペインでは、スペイン語のほかにもカタルーニャ語、ガリシア語、バスク語、バレンシア語などの公用語が認められています。英語力に関しては他のヨーロッパ諸国に比べて抜きんでているとはいえませんが、近年は不況も手伝って英語力強化に乗り出しています。スペイン語話者の英語の一般的な特徴は、母音の長短の区別が曖昧なこと（ship/sheep が同じ発音）、/h/ 音が脱落しやすいこと、/v/ が /b/ となるなどが挙げられます。またスペイン語には語頭に sp, st, sc などの組み合わせがないので、語頭に /e/ が挿入されることがあります（例 espain, eschool, estore）。なおスペイン語の標準語ともいうべきカスティーリャ方言には英語の /th/ に近い発音があります。

 Personal Interview

Read about Elena before you watch the interview of her.
エレナさんについて以下の情報を読み、インタビューを見ましょう。

Speaker Profile

Name	Elena
Age	51
Hometown	Numancia de la Sagra
Family	Single

 Elena's English ここに注意！
エレナさんの英語では、usually がユーシュアリーというように聞こえます。また of course, admire, leaders など、母音の後の /r/ 音は、イギリス標準英語と同じくほとんど発音されていません。

Check Your Understanding

Watch the video and do the following exercise.
映像を見て、以下の問いに答えなさい。

1. For breakfast Elena usually eats…
   a. lots of vegetables.
   b. pastries and coffee.
   c. a light meal.

2. What kind of person does Elena admire most?
   a. A person from India
   b. Political leaders
   c. Spiritual and peaceful leaders

3. Elena's future dream will come true when…
   a. she lives to be over 90 years old.
   b. all the old things in the world become renewed.
   c. everyone in the world has a better life.

4. How does Elena stay healthy?
   a. She exercises a lot.
   b. She eats a healthy breakfast.
   c. She lives in a small village to reduce her stress.

On Your Own

Discuss the following questions with your partner.
あなたもパートナーと話し合ってみましょう。

1. Which cities in Japan best represent the historical culture and modern culture of Japan and why?
2. Which Spanish foods introduced in the video do you want to try? Why?

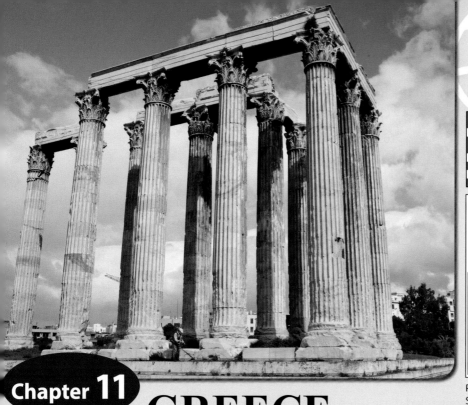

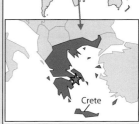
Crete

Population: 10.7 million
Size: 131,957 km²
Capital: Athens ☆
Currency: Euro

Chapter 11
GREECE

ヨーロッパ文化発祥の地ともいえるギリシャ。この章ではアテネの遺跡などから古代ギリシャ人の生活に迫ります。ゼウスを始めとしてギリシャ神話に登場する神々の名前が英語でどう発音されているか、ぜひ注意して聞いてみてください。

🌐 Warm-up Exercise

Complete the following exercise before continuing with the chapter.
この章の内容に入る前に、以下について考えてみましょう。

1. The official name of Greece in English is _____.
    a. The Republic of Olympia   **b.** Greco Europa
    c. The Hellenic Republic   **d.** Democratic Grecia

2. What was the occupation of the first recorded champion of the ancient Olympics?
    a. Farmer   **b.** Soldier   **c.** Doctor   **d.** Cook

3. The most popular cheese in Greece is _____ cheese.
    a. Feta   **b.** Gouda
    c. Mozzarella   **d.** Bleu

4. For five minutes, share as much as you know about Greece with your partner.

 **Vocabulary Exercise**

The following words appear in the Reading. Match the correct definition to each word.
次の単語は Reading で使われています。それぞれの単語の意味を a 〜 e から選びなさい。

1. respectively (   )   **a.** to suddenly flow out
2. aspect   (   )   **b.** to choose or take as one's own
3. gush   (   )   **c.** opposite or contrary in direction or action
4. conversely   (   )   **d.** nature, quality, character
5. adopt   (   )   **e.** precisely in the order given, sequentially

 **Reading** DL 22  CD 22

Greek Gods

Mythology is the study of myths. Myths are traditional stories told to explain historical events, beliefs, practices, and/or natural phenomenon. In Greek mythology, the world was divided into three parts: the sky, the sea, and the underworld. And the gods Zeus, Poseidon, and Hades **respectively** ruled these three parts. But there were many other gods, and each was
5 associated with a particular **aspect** of life and had many fantastic abilities. Many Greek myths tell of the relationships and conflicts between the gods as well as between gods and humans.

One myth tells us how the people of Athens tried to decide which god to choose as their god for the city. The people announced to Poseidon and Athena that they would choose the god who gave them the best gift. On top of the Acropolis, Poseidon took his trident, the source
10 of his power, and pushed it into the ground and a spring immediately **gushed** out. But the water was sea water. Athena, right next to the spring, gave the people an olive tree. The people thought the olive tree was a better gift, so they chose Athena to be their patron goddess of the city.

The ancient Greeks believed that if they didn't worship a particular god, bad things would
15 happen. **Conversely**, regular worship ensured good things happened. To avoid any jealousy between the gods, the Greeks tried to worship all of them equally. That is why you will find many temple remains dedicated to the different gods all over Greece today. But the presence of Greek gods is not limited to Greece. The Romans **adopted** many of
20 the same gods though they gave them different names; Zeus, Poseidon, and Hades became Jupiter, Neptune, and Pluto. These and other Greek gods became the subjects of many art and literary works, including Hollywood movies.

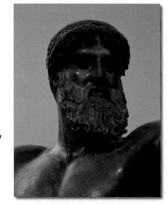

Notes

Acropolis 「アクロポリス（古代ギリシャ都市（ポリス）の中核の丘）」 trident 「（ギリシャ神話海神ポセイドンの）三叉のほこ」 spring 「泉」

 **Reading Comprehension**

Complete the following exercise.

Reading の内容と合うように 1 〜 5 の空欄に英語を書き入れなさい。

1. The god Hades was the ruler of the _____.

2. How did the people of Athens decide which god to choose for their city?

   _____

3. Poseidon pushed his _____ into the _____ and water gushed
   out.

4. Why did the ancient Greeks worship so many gods at the same time?

   _____

5. Zeus was called _____ by the Romans.

Part I

 GETTING TO KNOW GREECE    online video

 Vocabulary Preview   DL 23 ⊙ CD 23

Before watching the video, study the vocabulary below.

映像に出てくる語彙を確認しておきましょう。

1.	Temple of Zeus	ゼウス神殿
2.	Temple of Hephaestus	ヘファイストス神殿
3.	Theater of Dionysus	ディオニソス劇場
4.	Parthenon	パルテノン神殿
5.	Pnyx	プニュクス（アテネ中心部の丘の古代ギリシャ語での呼称）
6.	tribute	貢物をする
7.	Temple of Poseidon	ポセイドン神殿
8.	Crete	クレタ島
9.	authentic	本物の
10.	Minoan	ミノア（古代クレタ文明）の
11.	lentil	ヒラマメ、レンズマメ
12.	coriander	コリアンダー（タイではパクチーと呼ばれる香辛料）

Answer the following questions based on the video.
映像を見て、以下の問いに答えなさい。

1. Which is true about ancient sites in Athens?
    a. The Temple of Zeus has been given special honors.
    b. The Theater of Dionysus is the biggest attraction in Athens.
    c. The Parthenon stands forty feet high.
    d. The Pnyx is where ancient Greek citizens debated social issues and policies.

2. Which is true about Athena?
    a. She is the daughter of Poseidon.
    b. Her statue in the Parthenon was made of marble.
    c. She is the goddess of justice among others.
    d. The Acropolis in Athens was dedicated to her.

3. Which of the following does Scott NOT mention as something that can be learned from ancient Greek pottery?
    a. Literature
    b. Mythology
    c. Lifestyles
    d. Historical events

4. In cooking Minoan style food, Scott's friend Jerolyn…
    a. borrowed real ancient pots and jars for cooking.
    b. used only ingredients from Minoa.
    c. made an ancient style oven.
    d. tried to recreate the food ancient Greeks ate.

 **Second Viewing** *Focus on the details*

Watch the video again and choose the correct answer.
もう一度映像を見て、（　　）内の適切な言葉を選びなさい。

1. The (Temple of Hephaestus / Parthenon) was completed in 432 BCE.
2. The Parthenon is located (on top / in front) of the Acropolis.
3. In ancient Athens, male citizens debated politics a few times a (month / year).
4. When voting, a (white / black) stone indicated "yes."
5. Poseidon is the god of the (mountain / sea).
6. The period from 500 to 300 BCE is known as the (golden / cultural) age of Greece.
7. Jerolyn is an anthropologist, archeologist, and (potter / painter).
8. (Coriander / Honey) is an ingredient which was a Near Eastern import.

 Part II ▶ **ENGLISH IN GREECE** online video

ギリシャの公用語はギリシャ語。ギリシャ語はラテン語とともに長い間ヨーロッパで教養言語として学習され、他の言語へ大きな影響を与えてきました。 "It's all Greek to me" とは「ちんぷんかんぷんだ」という意味の英語の慣用表現ですし、一般にギリシャ語は難しいというイメージがありますが、英語にはギリシャ語を語源とする語彙が多数含まれています。ギリシャは EU のメンバーであり、外国語の知識は就職にも有利であるため、英語をはじめとして他言語を学習しようとする意欲は高まっています（英語も 9 歳から必修科目）。なお、ギリシャ語話者の英語の音声には、/h/ や /r/ 音が強く発音される、/ʃ/ の音が /s/ になる（she が see と発音される）、鼻濁音の前の /s/ が /z/ になる(smile が zmile と発音される)といった傾向が見られます。

 Personal Interview

Read about Eleni before you watch the interview of her.
エレーニさんについて以下の情報を読み、インタビューを見ましょう。

Speaker Profile

Name	Eleni
Age	28
Hometown	Pachia Ammos (Crete)
Family	Single

 Eleni's English ここに注意！
エレーニさんの英語で何と言っても特徴的なのは、/r/ 音が強く発音されているところでしょう。また I am coming や living など通常現在形が使われるところに、進行形が使われているところがあります。

Check Your Understanding

Watch the video and do the following exercise.
映像を見て、以下の問いに答えなさい。

1. Why does Eleni say that the kids are the best part of her job?
   a. Because they trust her.
   b. Because they learn so much.
   c. Because they are so innocent.

2. Which did Eleni NOT mention as the best part of Greece?
   a. Music and dance
   b. Food and people
   c. Sea and mountains

3. What does Eleni do to stay healthy?
   a. Listening to music
   b. Sleeping
   c. Nothing

4. Which is NOT true about Eleni's favorite food Pastitsio?
   a. It is made with lentils and honey.
   b. It has meat and spaghetti.
   c. It is baked in the oven.

On Your Own

Discuss the following questions with your partner.
あなたもパートナーと話し合ってみましょう。

1. What mythical stories from Japanese history do you know?
2. If you could try some food from a period of Japanese history (e.g., Nara period, Edo period, etc.), which period and food would you choose? Why?

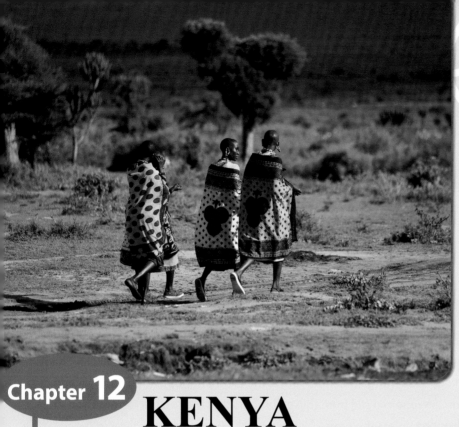

Population: 45 million
Size: 580,367 km²
Capital: Nairobi ☆
Currency: Kenyan Shilling

Chapter 12

KENYA

サバンナで伝統的な生活を送るマサイ族や野生動物が見られる広大な自然のイメージが強い
ケニアですが、この章では、人間も動物もそれぞれに一日の暮らしを精一杯に生きている様
子を見てみてください。

🌐 Warm-up Exercise

Complete the following exercise before continuing with the chapter.
この章の内容に入る前に、以下について考えてみましょう。

1. What does "safari" mean in Swahili?
   a. Danger   **b.** Jungle   **c.** Journey   **d.** Lions

2. What is the main staple food in Kenya?
   a. Ugali   **b.** Roti   **c.** Matoke   **d.** Couscous

3. Whose father is from Kenya?
   a. Nelson Mandela
   b. Martin Luther King Jr.
   c. Barack Obama
   d. Michael Jackson

4. For five minutes, share as much as you
   know about Kenya with your partner.

The following words appear in the Reading. Match the correct definition to each word.
次の単語は Reading で使われています。それぞれの単語の意味を a 〜 e から選びなさい。

1. poaching   (   )   **a.** marked by bad fortune or tragic fate
2. extermination (   )   **b.** to make impure or unsuitable by adding unclean things
3. imminent   (   )   **c.** complete destruction or elimination
4. contaminate (   )   **d.** illegal hunting
5. doomed   (   )   **e.** likely to occur soon

 **Reading**    DL 24   CD 24

Elephant Extermination

   One hundred! That is the number of elephants that will be killed in Africa today, tomorrow, and every day this year. A recent study reports from 2010 through 2012, over 100,000 elephants were killed, 80% by illegal **poaching**. In Central Africa, the elephant population has declined 64% in the last decade. Anyone can see from these numbers that the total **extermination** of
5 wild elephants is **imminent** unless the desire for ivory products is eliminated.

   In Africa, hunters can get as much as $200 per kg of ivory: nearly a year's income in some African countries. By the time an elephant tusk goes through middlemen, smugglers, and sellers, it will sell for as much as $2,000 per kg in Asia. Ivory is big business and has become a source of income for organized crime syndicates and militant groups.

10   Hunters often use automatic assault rifles, but those are expensive and noisy. Now the preferred method is poisoning the elephants' food or water hole. The **contaminated** food or water kills not just elephants but zebras, giraffes, and other animals as well. In addition, animals that eat the dead carcass of a poisoned elephant will also die.

15   Despite the 1989 international ban on ivory trade, efforts to stop the problem have failed. Ineffective laws, lax punishment, and corrupt officials are to blame. However, the root of the problem is consumer demand. Tons of illegal ivory ends up in Asia to be carved
20 into ornaments, jewelry, religious items, and name seals. Unless people stop desiring and purchasing ivory products, the elephant is **doomed** to follow the mammoth.

Notes

tusk「ゾウなどの牙」 middleman「中間商人、ブローカー」 smuggler「密輸業者」 organized crime syndicate「暴力団」 automatic assault rifle「自動突撃ライフル」 carcass「動物などの死体」 lax「厳しくない、手ぬるい」

🌐 Reading Comprehension

Complete the following exercise.
Reading の内容と合うように 1 〜 5 の空欄に英語を書き入れなさい。

1. How many elephants are killed in Africa every day?

   _____

2. The price of 1 kg of ivory increases _____ times when it goes from Africa to Asia.

3. The ivory business has become a source of income for _____
   _____ _____ and _____ groups.

4. When an elephant dies from poisoning, what additional problems does this create?

   _____

5. What is the root of the problem?

   _____

Part I

▶ GETTING TO KNOW KENYA

online / video

🌐 Vocabulary Preview

🎧 DL 25 ⊙ CD 25

Before watching the video, study the vocabulary below.
映像に出てくる語彙を確認しておきましょう。

1. tribe   部族
2. poverty   貧困
3. flash flood   鉄砲水、急激な増水
4. game reserve   動物保護区、禁猟区（game とは猟の獲物を意味する）
5. cub   ライオン（クマ、トラなど）の子ども

Answer the following questions based on the video.
映像を見て、以下の問いに答えなさい。

1. Which is NOT mentioned as one of the reasons life is difficult in Kenya?
   a. Wars
   b. Poverty
   c. Unemployment
   d. Weather

2. Flash floods…
   a. occur because of poorly planned roads.
   b. are the worst in rural areas.
   c. must be watched out for every minute of every day.
   d. can be powerful enough to wash out bridges.

3. Scott introduces giraffes and lions mainly to…
   a. explain the beauty of natural environment in Kenya.
   b. give examples of the struggles animals face in Kenya.
   c. promote the national parks and game reserves in Kenya.
   d. show the impact of human conflicts on animals in Kenya.

4. Which is true about lions?
   a. Only female lions and their cubs live in groups.
   b. Lions hunt only at night.
   c. Lions hunt but they also steal food from other animals.
   d. Once they eat, lions will not hunt for two weeks.

 **Second Viewing** *Focus on the details*

Watch the video again and choose the correct answer.
もう一度映像を見て、（　　）内の適切な言葉を選びなさい。

1. Visitors in Kenya will become (tired / aware) of the struggle for existence.
2. (Having many tribes in the country / Being surrounded by many countries) is one cause of conflicts in Kenya that Scott mentions.
3. (About half / Three-quarters) of the population lives on less than $1.25 per day.
4. The (literacy / unemployment) rate is 40% in Kenya.
5. Flash floods are at (worst / best) an inconvenience.
6. Giraffes spend much of the day (sleeping / eating).
7. (Giraffes / Lions) eat 40-50 pounds at one time.
8. An adult (male / female) lion is about six feet long and weighs 400 pounds.

 Part II **ENGLISH IN KENYA** online/video

ケニア共和国には、40 以上もの言語が存在しますが、公用語はスワヒリ語と英語。スワヒリ語以外の言語を母語とするケニア人も多数いますが、スワヒリ語は「国語」と認識されています。けれどもケニアで社会的ステータスを持ち政治やビジネス、教育の場で使われているのは旧宗主国イギリスのことば、英語です。ただし、ケニアの英語には強勢の位置の変化（photógraphy を photográphy と発音）、有声子音と無声子音の混同（cake を gake, bakery を pakery と発音）、有声子音の前の鼻濁音の付加（bad を mbad, goat を ngoat と発音）といった特徴が見られます。

 Personal Interview

Read about Ephram before you watch the interview of him.
エフラムさんについて以下の情報を読み、インタビューを見ましょう。

Speaker Profile

Name	Ephram Kinyua Murithi
Age	39
Hometown	Githure
Family	Married

 Ephram's English ここに注意！

エフラムさんの英語では、research がリサーチャのように語末の子音に母音のア /ə/ が追加されたり、hard の /h/ 音が脱落したりしています。また、potatoes がどのように発音されているか注意してみてください。

Check Your Understanding

Watch the video and do the following exercise.
映像を見て、以下の問いに答えなさい。

1. What advice does Ephram have for university students?
   a. To concentrate on research
   b. To become smart enough to work
   c. To pass exams as fast as they can

2. Using Facebook and Twitter is…
   a. Ephram's image of Japan.
   b. one of Kenya's biggest social trends.
   c. a necessity for a finance manager in Kenya.

3. What does Ephram recommend visitors see or do in Kenya?
   a. To visit Maasai Mara
   b. To eat Nyama Choma, the roasted meat
   c. To hunt the biggest animals in the world

4. Which tribe does he belong to?
   a. Nakuru   **b.** Maasai   **c.** Kikuyu

On Your Own

Discuss the following questions with your partner.
あなたもパートナーと話し合ってみましょう。

1. What skills do you think are most useful in order to live well
   a) in nature, b) in Japan, and c) in the global world?

2. What do you think are the biggest struggles for people in Japan and in the world,
   between the ages of a) 13-20, b) 20-30, and c) 60-80?

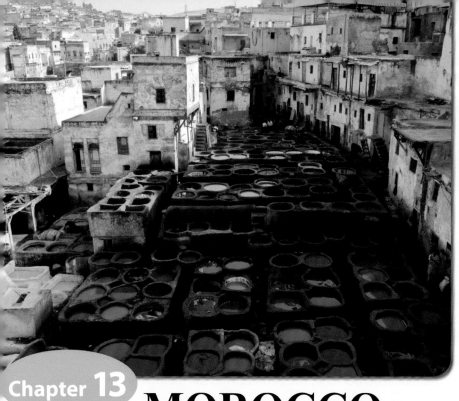

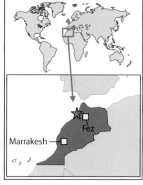

Population: 32.9 million
Size: 446,550 km²
Capital: Rabat ☆
Currency: Moroccan Dirham

Chapter 13

MOROCCO

モロッコは、ラクダに乗ってサハラ砂漠を旅したり、迷路のようなアラブのマーケットで買い物をしたりなど、映画で見るような場面を体験することができる国です。この章では、ベルベル人の伝統食や昔ながらの職人芸について学んでください。

🌐 Warm-up Exercise

Complete the following exercise before continuing with the chapter.
この章の内容に入る前に、以下について考えてみましょう。

1. What is Morocco known to Arabs as?
   - **a.** The Red City
   - **b.** Sahara Kingdom
   - **c.** The Gateway to Africa
   - **d.** The Land of the Setting Sun

2. What is the most popular tea in Morocco?
   - **a.** Ginger tea
   - **b.** Mint tea
   - **c.** Butter tea
   - **d.** Barley tea

3. What is Japan's number one food import from Morocco?
   - **a.** Octopus
   - **b.** Shrimp
   - **c.** Eel
   - **d.** Crab

4. For five minutes, share as much as you know about Morocco with your partner.

 **Vocabulary Exercise**

The following words appear in the Reading. Match the correct definition to each word.
次の単語は Reading で使われています。それぞれの単語の意味を a 〜 e から選びなさい。

1. herding （　　）　**a.** to slowly cook in water just below boiling
2. evidence （　　）　**b.** designed or adapted for actual use
3. savory　（　　）　**c.** keeping and raising a number of animals that graze
4. simmer　（　　）　**d.** something that makes plain or clear, proves
5. practical （　　）　**e.** pleasant, agreeable in taste or smell

 **Reading**

DL 26　CD 26

A Dish of Lifestyle

If you went to Italy, you would naturally eat pasta. If you traveled to Japan, sushi would be the course for at least one meal. In Morocco, you must eat tajine.

Tajine actually is a traditional Berber food. The Berbers, who call themselves "Imazighen" meaning the free people, are indigenous groups of people scattered across North Africa. Their
5　history goes back 4,000 years to when they existed on light agriculture and sheep or goat **herding**. Some groups of Berbers also became merchants, establishing trade routes across North Africa. Today 40% of Moroccans are of Berber decent.

Evidence of their lifestyle is reflected in the tajine dish. Tajine is made with a variety of vegetables and strips of meat. Mutton, beef, chicken, and even fish are common varieties of
10　tajine. As for vegetables, potatoes, carrots, and peas are frequently added, but just about any vegetable available could go into the pot.

The real secret to **savory** tajine is the herbs, spices, and dried fruit added. Merchants traveling across North Africa and later the Mediterranean would be introduced to a wide variety of spices. Thus, it is not surprising that a typical tajine is cooked with
15　paprika, cumin, saffron, parsley, ginger, salt, pepper, honey, dates, and more.

Even the unique tajine cooking pot tells us about its origin. Its signature feature is the cone-shaped top. This design causes steam to collect on the sides and roll back into the pot, making it possible
20　to slowly **simmer** the cheaper or tougher cuts of meat until they are tender and juicy. This recycling of the water is very **practical** in areas where water is in short supply.

Even if you are not entertained by the historical and cultural background of tajine, you will enjoy this delicious Moroccan favorite.

Notes

tajine「タジン鍋（北アフリカの鍋料理）」　Berber「ベルベル族（の）」　cumin「クミン（香辛料）」　date「ナツメヤシの実」　signature「特製の、代表的な、目玉となる」

Reading Comprehension

Complete the following exercise.

Reading の内容と合うように 1 〜 5 の空欄に英語を書き入れなさい。

1. What do the Berber people call themselves?

    _____

2. Besides agriculture and raising goats and sheep, some Berber people became

    _____.

3. Agriculture and raising goats and sheep are reflected in tajine by the

    _____ and _____ ingredients.

4. What is the real secret to delicious tajine?

    _____

5. The cone shape of the lid causes steam to collect and _____ _____

    _____ the pot.

Part I

GETTING TO KNOW MOROCCO

online / video

Vocabulary Preview

 DL 27 CD 27

Before watching the video, study the vocabulary below.

映像に出てくる語彙を確認しておきましょう。

1. earthen 　　　土の、陶器の
2. tannery 　　　皮なめし工場、革工場（tanning は皮なめし）
3. medina 　　　メディナ（北アフリカの多くの都市にある旧市街を指す）
4. quicklime 　　生石灰
5. cow urine 　　牛の尿
6. hide 　　　　獣の皮
7. dung 　　　　ふん

Answer the following questions based on the video.
映像を見て、以下の問いに答えなさい。

1. What does Scott say about Morocco?
   a. Technology is slowly spreading in this country.
   b. Many jobs people had 10 years ago no longer exist.
   c. Morocco is trying to be a modern country.
   d. Many things are still done in a traditional way.

2. Which is NOT mentioned as an example of traditional life?
   a. Living in mud houses
   b. Raising cows
   c. Making breads
   d. Making rugs

3. Which is true about leather making in Morocco?
   a. Leather is one of Morocco's largest exports.
   b. Only high quality leather is hand-made nowadays.
   c. There are hundreds of tanneries in the city of Fez.
   d. Many tanneries in Fez are famous for using the traditional method.

4. Henna...
   a. is a native plant of India.
   b. is easy for anyone to do well.
   c. needs to be mixed with lemon to make it into a paste.
   d. has been used for thousands of years.

 **Second Viewing** *Focus on the details*

Watch the video again and choose the correct answer.
もう一度映像を見て、（　　）内の適切な言葉を選びなさい。

1. Scott feels that (changes occur at an accelerating pace / time seems to have stopped) in some parts of Morocco.

2. Home-made (flat / fat) breads are baked in earthen ovens.

3. Scott mentions high quality (rugs / houses) are also hand-made in Morocco.

4. Traditional tanneries soak the skins in a mixture of water, (salt / malt), quicklime, and cow urine.

5. To (soften / dye) the hides, pigeon dung is used.

6. The leather must stay in a colored dye for (2 to 3 days / a week).

7. The final process of tanning the leather is (scraping and trimming / stretching and drying) the leather.

8. The coating of lemon and sugar helps (the henna dry faster / protect the henna).

 Part II ▶ **ENGLISH IN MOROCCO** (online/video)

モロッコの公用語はアラビア語とタマジグト（ベルベル）語。モロッコでは標準アラビア語とはかなり異なるダリジャと呼ばれるモロッコ方言が使われています。タマジグトはベルベル人の日常言語です。モロッコはフランスの保護領だったため多くの人がフランス語を話し、また一部はスペインの支配下にもあったため、スペイン語も有力な外国語です。英語の浸透度は高いとはいえませんが、社会的成功の手段となっており、今後学習すべき言語として強く意識されています。なおモロッコの人々の英語の音声の特徴は（母語にもよりますが）、/p/ が /b/ と発音されやすいこと、/r/ 音が強く発音されること、そして /ʒ/ の音が /dʒ/ と発音される傾向があることなどが挙げられます。

 Personal Interview

Read about Adil before you watch the interview of him.
アディルさんについて以下の情報を読み、インタビューを見ましょう。

Speaker Profile

Name	Adil
Age	23
Hometown	Asilah
Family	Single

 Adil's English ここに注意！

言語学を学んでいるというアディルさんの英語は全体的にアメリカ式に近い発音です。… years old**a** というように語末の子音にア /ə/ の音がついたり、how の /h/ 音が脱落してアウに聞こえるところが注意点です。

Check Your Understanding

Watch the video and do the following exercise.
映像を見て、以下の問いに答えなさい。

1. Who does Adil want to have coffee with?
   a. Prophet Muhammad
   b. Prime Minister of Morocco
   c. Product Manager

2. What does Adil say is the best thing about Morocco?
   a. The cultural food
   b. The cultural part of Moroccan language
   c. The cultural diversity

3. What does Adil want to be in the future?
   a. A graphic designer
   b. An English textbook designer
   c. An English translator

4. What does Adil do to relax besides reading?
   a. Jogging   b. Ball juggling   c. Jumping rope

On Your Own

Discuss the following questions with your partner.
あなたもパートナーと話し合ってみましょう。

1. Do you like leather products? Why or why not?
2. What did you think about the henna skin decoration? Do you like decorating your skin? If you got a tattoo, what would it be or look like?

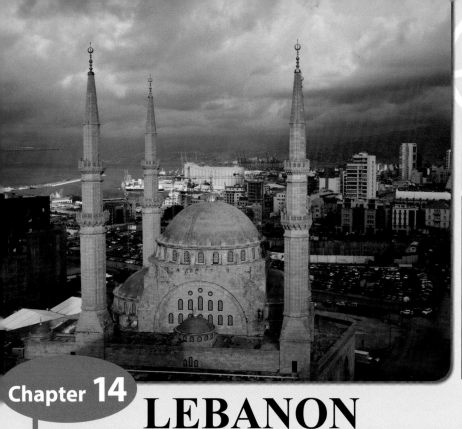

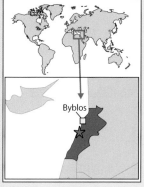

Population: 5.8 million
Size: 10,400 km²
Capital: Beirut ☆
Currency: Lebanese Pound

Chapter 14

LEBANON

中東の小国レバノンは、古代フェニキア人が都市国家を建設し、地中海貿易で活躍した場所です。その後も様々な民族がレバノンの歴史を彩っています。この章では、「樹木」を通してレバノンの歴史文化に触れてみましょう。

🌐 Warm-up Exercise

Complete the following exercise before continuing with the chapter.
この章の内容に入る前に、以下について考えてみましょう。

1. What is the official language of Lebanon?
   a. Arabic   **b.** English   **c.** Farsi   **d.** French

2. Which country has the highest number of Lebanese descendents?
   a. Britian   **b.** Brazil   **c.** France   **d.** United States

3. All of the following celebrities are part Lebanese
   EXCEPT _____.
   a. Salma Hayek   **b.** Shakira
   c. Carlos Ghosn   **d.** Natalie Portman

4. For five minutes, share as much as you
   know about Lebanon with your partner.

The following words appear in the Reading. Match the correct definition to each word.
次の単語は Reading で使われています。それぞれの単語の意味を a～e から選びなさい。

1. aspire　　　（　　）　**a.** connected or related to the sea
2. monopoly　（　　）　**b.** to spread or scatter
3. maritime　（　　）　**c.** the beginning or start
4. disseminate（　　）　**d.** to desire or seek, especially for something of higher value
5. inception　（　　）　**e.** exclusive control of a commodity, service, or market

 **Reading**

 DL 28　CD 28

Origins of the ABC's

　　Naturally, once humans learned to speak they next **aspired** to write. Cuneiform and Egyptian hieroglyphs are some of the oldest writing systems created, dating back to 3000 BCE. These writing systems are no longer used. However, today we still use something the Phoenicians created: the alphabet.

5　　The Phoenicians were ancient people who lived along the eastern Mediterranean coast in what is now Lebanon and Syria. Because of the **monopoly** they had on trading a purple dye, they became known as the purple people or "Phoinikes" in Greek from which we get the name Phoenicians. The Phoenicians were shipbuilders and had a strong **maritime** economy at the city of Byblos. Shipping and trading took them all over the Mediterranean especially Egypt

10　and Greece. This helped **disseminate** the Phoenician alphabet to other countries. They traded Lebanese Cedar trees for Egyptian papyrus to write on. Because of damp weather conditions in Lebanon including fog, rain, and even snow, papyrus rotted and few written examples of the Phoenician alphabet survived. The oldest example of the alphabet we have was carved onto a stone sarcophagus.

15　　Most sources cite the 15th century BCE as the time of the alphabet's **inception** when the Phoenicians created it. The Phoenician alphabet consists of 22 consonants and no vowels. It was assumed that readers, knowing the language, would fill in the correct vowel sounds. It was written horizontally right to left, and originally there were no spaces

20　between the words. In later developments, slashes or dots were used between words. Eventually, the Greeks added their vowels to the Phoenician alphabet. The Greek alphabet is the origin of the Latin alphabet, which is what you are using now, to read this passage.

Notes

cuneiform 「楔形文字(くさびがたもじ)」　hieroglyph 「神聖（象形）文字」　Phoenicians 「フェニキア人」　Lebanese Cedar 「レバノン杉」　damp 「湿った」　rot 「腐る」　sarcophagus 「石棺」

Reading Comprehension

Complete the following exercise.
Reading の内容と合うように 1 ～ 5 の空欄に英語を書き入れなさい。

1. _____ and _____ _____ are writing systems no longer used.

2. Why were the Phoenicians called the purple people?
   _____

3. The Phoenicians traded _____ _____ _____ to get Egyptian papyrus.

4. Why are there few examples of the Phoenician alphabet today?
   _____

5. The Greeks use the Phoenician alphabet but added their _____ to it.

Part I

 GETTING TO KNOW LEBANON online/video

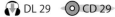 **Vocabulary Preview** 🎧 DL 29 ◎ CD 29

Before watching the video, study the vocabulary below.
映像に出てくる語彙を確認しておきましょう。

1.	Fertile Crescent	肥沃な三日月地帯（古代オリエント文明の中心地）
2.	vat	液体貯蔵用の大きな桶、タンク
3.	ground-up	すりつぶした、挽いた
4.	inscription	碑銘、碑文
5.	King Ahiram	ビブロス（Byblos）の王アヒラム（紀元前 1000 頃）
6.	resin	樹脂
7.	grove	木立、小さい森

Answer the following questions based on the video.
映像を見て、以下の問いに答えなさい。

1. Which is NOT true about Lebanon?
   a. It is a small country.
   b. It is located on the western edge of the Mediterranean Sea.
   c. It is part of the area called the Fertile Crescent.
   d. It is part of the area where the olive tree originates from.

2. Which is true about the Saifan family?
   a. They have been making soap for centuries.
   b. Their soap making is recorded in history.
   c. Their soap is made of 100% natural olive oil.
   d. They make 4,000 kg of soap per year.

3. According to Scott, what is the most important contribution of the Phoenicians?
   a. The alphabet
   b. The Sarcophagus of King Ahiram
   c. Ship building
   d. Soap making

4. Which is NOT true about Lebanese Cedars?
   a. They are deeply connected to Lebanese history.
   b. They were used to build Phoenician ships.
   c. They are mentioned in religious texts.
   d. They were all cut down before the 19th century.

 **Second Viewing** *Focus on the details*

Watch the video again and choose the correct answer.
もう一度映像を見て、（　　）内の適切な言葉を選びなさい。

1. The (Mediterranean / Fertile Crescent) is where civilization began.
2. The olive branch is a symbol of (victory / peace).
3. At Saifan, soap flakes are (softened / air-dried) for three months.
4. Soap is ground-up and rolled four times to (make it extra smooth / remove 20% of water).
5. The city of Byblos was an early (Phoenician / Babylonian) settlement.
6. The earliest existing example of the Phoenician (alphabet / king) dates back to 1000 BCE.
7. Cedar resin was used for (fragrance / mummification) in Egypt.
8. On the Lebanese flag, the (olive / cedar) tree is depicted.

ENGLISH IN LEBANON

online video

> レバノンは人口の 95% がアラブ人で（残りはアルメニア人）、イスラム教の国というイメージが強いですが、キリスト教徒も国民の4割にのぼります。残念ながら宗教的対立やイスラエルやシリアを始めとする周辺国家の干渉などにより内紛が絶えず、多くのレバノン人が海外に脱出しています。レバノンの公用語はアラビア語ですが、日常では標準アラビア語ではなくレバノン方言が使われています。また、フランスの植民地だったことから現時点では英語よりもフランス語が広く通じます。なお、レバノン方言には /p/, /v/ の音がなく、外来語のみに使用されるため、/b/, /f/ で代用されることがあります。

 Personal Interview

Read about Nadine before you watch the interview of her.
ナディーンさんについて以下の情報を読み、インタビューを見ましょう。

Speaker Profile

Name	Nadine
Age	29
Hometown	Beirut
Family	Single

Nadine's English ここに注意！
ナディーンさんの英語は、**well, people** や **single** など語末の /l/ の音がやや強く発音されているところがあります。

Check Your Understanding

Watch the video and do the following exercise.
映像を見て、以下の問いに答えなさい。

1. What does Nadine say is the best thing about Lebanon?
   a. It is a peaceful and loving country.
   b. There are so many places to visit.
   c. You can travel anywhere in the country in a few hours.

2. Why does Nadine want to have coffee with Kahlil Gibran?
   a. Because he is from Lebanon.
   b. Because he has big knowledge.
   c. Because he loves nature.

3. How did Nadine mainly learn English?
   a. From music and movies
   b. At French school
   c. By writing in English

4. What is Nadine's favorite food?
   a. Any type of food
   b. Home-made food with love
   c. Whatever she made herself

On Your Own

Discuss the following questions with your partner.
あなたもパートナーと話し合ってみましょう。

1. What kind of tree do you think is highly valued in Japan and why? (e.g., cherry tree, pine tree, maple (*kaede*) tree, *hinoki* tree, etc.)? What is your favorite tree?

2. In the future, because of technology or globalization, do you think there will be a new (universal) writing script?

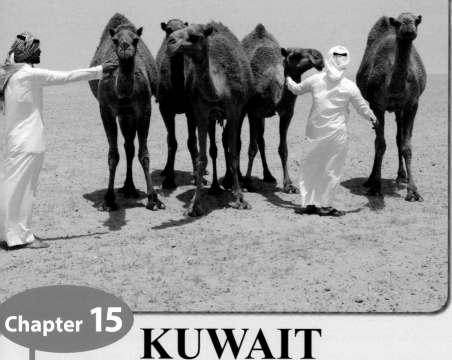

Population: 3.9 million
Size: 17,818 km²
Capital: Kuwait City ★
Currency: Kuwaiti Dinar

Chapter 15

KUWAIT

クウェートは 1990 年にイラクから侵攻を受けるなど一時は危機に陥りましたが、オイルマネーで潤う富裕国です。一方、砂漠気候やイスラムの戒律など、生活環境は私たちにとってはやや厳しいと感じられるかもしれません。

🌐 Warm-up Exercise

Complete the following exercise before continuing with the chapter.
この章の内容に入る前に、以下について考えてみましょう。

1. What percentage of Kuwaiti people work for the government or government related businesses?

   a. 34%   **b.** 54%   **c.** 74%   **d.** 94%

2. Based on per capita GDP, Kuwait is the _____ richest country in the world.

   a. 3rd   **b.** 5th   **c.** 7th   **d.** 9th

3. Women in Kuwait were allowed to vote for the first time in _____.

   a. 1875   **b.** 1961

   c. 2000   **d.** 2005

4. For five minutes, share as much as you know about Kuwait with your partner.

 **Vocabulary Exercise**

The following words appear in the Reading. Match the correct definition to each word.
次の単語は Reading で使われています。それぞれの単語の意味を a ～ e から選びなさい。

1. clue ( ) **a.** decent, not being extravagant
2. norm ( ) **b.** hint, something that helps someone find something
3. pertinent ( ) **c.** a standard, model, or pattern regarded as typical
4. modest ( ) **d.** having influence over others, most common, main
5. predominant ( ) **e.** relating to the matter at hand, relevant, valid

 **Reading**

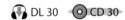 DL 30 CD 30

Desert Attire

Our clothes have many functions. Besides offering protection from the environment, our clothes give **clues** as to who we are and what our roles are in society. Fashion, aimed at making us look appealing, has now become a primary motivator in clothing, but clothes generally need to follow the **norms** of society. In Kuwait, traditional clothes also conform to religious beliefs. It's
5 still common nowadays to see Kuwaiti men and women wearing traditional Arab clothing on a daily basis.

Arab clothing is **pertinent** to the environment. Summer temperatures in Kuwait normally reach 110-120 F, so people wear traditional clothing which is lightweight and loose-fitting. Traditional clothing is also **modest** and simple because Islam, the **predominant** religion in
10 Kuwait, teaches that people should be modest and respectful.

Kuwaiti men wear a one-piece that extends from the shoulder to the toes called a *dishdasha*. Lightweight white or ivory material is used for the summer *dishdashas.* Winter *dishdashas* are heavier and come in gray or dark colors. The *gahfiya* is a knit cap that is covered with the *ghutra,* a large square cloth that
15 is folded into a triangle. It is all held on with a black cord called an *agal*. Long ago the *agal* also served as a rope to tie the camel's feet at night.

The *abaya* is the full-length long-sleeve dress worn by women. The aim is to cover everything. Traditionally in Kuwait the *abaya* was
20 loose-fitting and covered the head as well. Today the *abaya* may be a tailored fit with a belt at the waist and other accessories and embroideries. It may have a separate head covering called a *hijab*. Or often Kuwaiti women just wear the *hijab* to cover their hair.

Notes

dishdasha「ディスダーシャ（アラビア半島の男性の民族衣装）」 *gahfiya*「クーフィーヤ（布製のキャップ）」 *ghutra*「ゴトラ（男性用頭布）」 *agal*「アガール（縄）」 *abaya*「アバヤ（アラビア半島の女性の民族衣装）」 *hijab*「ヒジャブ（女性用頭布）」

 **Reading Comprehension**

Complete the following exercise.
Reading の内容と合うように 1 ～ 5 の空欄に英語を書き入れなさい。

1. What do clothes generally need to do?
   _____

2. Because of the warm temperatures, traditional clothing in Kuwait is
   _____ and _____.

3. What is the name of the traditional one-piece clothing for Kuwaiti men?
   _____

4. What was *agal* used for long ago at night?
   _____

5. The *hijab* is a _____ _____ for women.

Part I

▶ **GETTING TO KNOW KUWAIT**   online / video

  Vocabulary Preview   🎧 DL 31   💿 CD 31

Before watching the video, study the vocabulary below.
映像に出てくる語彙を確認しておきましょう。

1. Persian Gulf   ペルシャ湾
2. nomadic   遊牧民の
3. double eyelid   二重まぶた
4. Dhow ship   ダウ船（インド洋・アラビア海などの沿海貿易用の木造帆船）

Answer the following questions based on the video.
映像を見て、以下の問いに答えなさい。

1. Which is NOT true about Kuwait?
   a. It is on the Persian Gulf.
   b. It now has lots of oil.
   c. Most of the country is a desert.
   d. Pearls were discovered there in 1938.

2. According to Scott, why were camels important for survival long ago?
   a. Because they could easily find water.
   b. Because they provided food and transportation.
   c. Because they make good companions.
   d. Because they could be sold for lots of money.

3. The men who are building Dhow ships today are…
   a. originally from Africa and India.
   b. the descendants of Kuwaiti shipbuilders.
   c. the best in the region.
   d. changing the tradition by making models.

4. Kuwait produces…
   a. 7% of the world's oil needs.
   b. 3.4 million barrels of oil a month.
   c. nearly 30% of the world's oil supply.
   d. about 3 million barrels of oil a day.

 **Second Viewing** *Focus on the details*

Watch the video again and choose the correct answer.
もう一度映像を見て、（　　）内の適切な言葉を選びなさい。

1. Kuwait shares a border with (Iran / Iraq).
2. Kuwait is (smaller / bigger) than Shikoku.
3. Today camels are more important as a means of (transportation / investment).
4. Camels are called "the (star / ship) of the desert."
5. For centuries, Kuwaitis had a reputation as the best (shipbuilders / traders).
6. The men build model ships to preserve (the tradition / their reputation) for the future.
7. The Kuwaiti government owns (all / 70%) of the oil in the country.
8. A lot of oil money ends up in the hands of (foreigners / Kuwaiti people).

 Part II

▶ ENGLISH IN KUWAIT 　online / video

クウェートの公用語はアラビア語ですが、他のアラビア諸国と同じく日常会話には標準アラビア語とは異なるクウェート方言を使用しています。莫大な石油収入によりクウェートの国民は高い生活水準を維持できていますが、海外各国からの出稼ぎ労働者が国民の人口を上回るほど多数に上ります。そのため、国内におけるコミュニケーションにも英語が重要な役割を果たしています。もともとイギリスの植民地でもありましたが、クウェート国民もグローバル化を強く意識して英語教育にも余念がありません。アラブ語話者の英語の特徴としては /p/, /v/ が /b/, /f/ などと発音されることが挙げられます。（モロッコ、レバノンの章も参照。）

 Personal Interview

Read about Jenan before you watch the interview of her.
ジナンさんについて以下の情報を読み、インタビューを見ましょう。

Speaker Profile

Name	Jenan Al-Ebrahem
Age	19
Hometown	Kuwait City
Family	Single

 Jenan's English ここに注意！

ジナンさんの英語で特徴的なのは語末の /t/ にかすかに /s/ が追加されているところです。Kuwait(s), meat(s), almost(s), a lot(s) など、/t/ で終わる単語に注意して聞いてみてください。

Check Your Understanding

Watch the video and do the following exercise.
映像を見て、以下の問いに答えなさい。

1. Which is NOT a reason Jenan gives for liking the color pink?
    a. Pink is a cheerful color.
    b. She is a girl.
    c. All girls like pink.

2. What does Jenan say she is going to do in Dubai in the near future?
    a. She will go to a Machboos restaurant.
    b. She will buy an apartment there.
    c. She will study there.

3. Jenan doesn't have a pet because she...
    a. doesn't like all animals.
    b. is allergic to animals.
    c. is going to study in a university.

4. What does Jenan say about the *hijab*?
    a. All women should wear *hijab* in Kuwait.
    b. Not all women wear *hijab* in Kuwait.
    c. She wears a *hijab* almost every day.

On Your Own

Discuss the following questions with your partner.
あなたもパートナーと話し合ってみましょう。

1. If you knew you could receive large amounts of money anytime you wanted, how would that change your behavior and daily activities?
2. Considering what you read in the passage about the purpose of clothing, do you think Kuwaiti people will be wearing more western clothing in the future?

Resources

General Information

The World Factbook (CIA) [Last visited in 2014]
https://www.cia.gov/library/publications/the-world-factbook/

Selected References for World Englishes

Crystal, D. (2003). *English as a global language*. Cambridge University Press.

Ehrich, S., & Avery, P. (2013). *Teaching American English pronunciation*. Oxford University Press.

Ethnologue: Language of the World. www.ethnologue.com

Jenkins, J. (2003). *World Englishes: A resource book for students*. Routledge.

Kachru, B., Kachru, Y., & Nelson, C. (2009). *The Handbook of World Englishes*. Wiley-Blackwell.

Swan, M., & Smith, B. (2001). *Learner English: A teacher's guide to interference and other problems*. Cambridge University Press.

Trudgill, P., & Hannah, J. (2008). *International English: A guide to the varieties of standard English* (5th ed.). Routledge.

Walker, R. (2010). *Teaching the pronunciation of English as a Lingua Franca*. Oxford University Press.

For More Information

Scott & Soon Jeong: Nobis Traveling, Traveling the World
http://scottandsoonjeong.wordpress.com

Henna Café (Henna art, Morocco)
www.hennacafemarrakech.com

Minoan Tastes (Jerolyn Morrison's Minoan cooking business, Greece)
http://minoitongefseis.com
http://www.historicalcooking.com

Said Saifan Est. (Olive oil soap maker, Lebanon)
www.saifanest.com

Special Thanks to:

Michael, (Germany) Angsburger Hotel www.stadthotel-landsberg.de
Natalia, (Poland) Graphic Design Co. Merea www.merea.com.pl
Nadine, (Lebanon) NGO Ourqualia www.ourqualia.org

URLs above are as of October 2014.

このテキストのメインページ
www.kinsei-do.co.jp/plusmedia/413

次のページの QR コードを読み取ると
直接ページにジャンプできます

オンライン映像配信サービス「plus⁺Media」について

本テキストの映像は plus⁺Media ページ（www.kinsei-do.co.jp/plusmedia）から、ストリーミング再生でご利用いただけます。手順は以下に従ってください。

ログイン

● ご利用には、ログインが必要です。
サイトのログインページ（www.kinsei-do.co.jp/plusmedia/login）へ行き、plus⁺Media パスワード（次のページのシールをはがしたあとに印字されている数字とアルファベット）を入力します。

● パスワードは各テキストにつき 1 つです。
有効期限は、<u>はじめてログインした時点から 1 年間</u>になります。

ログインページ

[利用方法]

次のページにある QR コード、もしくは plus⁺Media トップページ（www.kinsei-do.co.jp/plusmedia）から該当するテキストを選んで、そのテキストのメインページにジャンプしてください。

メニューページ　　　　再生画面

plus+Media トップ　　　　メインページ

「Video」「Audio」をタッチすると、それぞれのメニューページにジャンプしますので、そこから該当する項目を選べば、ストリーミングが開始されます。

[推奨環境]

iOS (iPhone, iPad)	OS: iOS 6 〜 13 ブラウザ：標準ブラウザ	Android	OS: Android 4.x 〜 10.0 ブラウザ：標準ブラウザ、Chrome
PC	OS: Windows 7/8/8.1/10, MacOS X　ブラウザ：Internet Explorer 10/11, Microsoft Edge, Firefox 48以降, Chrome 53以降, Safari		

※最新の推奨環境についてはウェブサイトをご確認ください。
※上記の推奨環境を満たしている場合でも、機種によってはご利用いただけない場合もあります。また、推奨環境は技術動向等により変更される場合があります。予めご了承ください。

このシールをはがすと
plus+Media 利用のための
パスワードが
記載されています。

一度はがすと元に戻すことは
できませんのでご注意下さい。

◀ここからはがして下さい

4134
On Board for More
World Adventures
plus+Media®

本書には CD（別売）があります

On Board for More World Adventures
続・映像で学ぶ世界の文化と英語

2021 年 2 月 20 日 初版第 1 刷発行
2023 年 8 月 25 日 初版第 6 刷発行

編著者 Scott Berlin
小林 めぐみ

発行者 福 岡 正 人
発行所 株式会社 金星堂

（〒101-0051）東京都千代田区神田神保町 3-21
Tel.（03）3263-3828（営業部）
（03）3263-3997（編集部）
Fax（03）3263-0716
https://www.kinsei-do.co.jp

編集担当／四條雪菜　　　　　　　　Printed in Japan
印刷・製本所／大日本印刷株式会社

ISBN978-4-7647-4134-8　C1082